The SERMON on the MOUNT

A Study on
GOD'S UPSIDE-DOWN KINGDOM

KRISTIN SCHMUCKER

TABLE *of* CONTENTS

Study Suggestions..*Page 4*

Week One...*Page 6*

Week One Memory Verse......................................*Page 27*

Week One Reflection...*Page 28*

Week Two..*Page 30*

Week Two Memory Verse......................................*Page 50*

Week Two Reflection...*Page 52*

Week Three..*Page 54*

Week Three Memory Verse....................................*Page 75*

Week Three Reflection...*Page 76*

Week Four..*Page 78*

Week Four Memory Verse......................................*Page 98*

Week Four Reflection...*Page 100*

Week Five...*Page 102*

Week Five Memory Verse....................................*Page 123*

Week Five Reflection...*Page 124*

Week Six...*Page 126*

Week Six Memory Verse......................................*Page 146*

Week Six Reflection...*Page 148*

What is the Gospel?..*Page 150*

STUDY SUGGESTIONS

Thank you for choosing this study to help you dig into God's Word. We are so passionate about women getting into Scripture, and we are praying that this study will be a tool to help you do that. Here are a few tips to help you get the most from this study:

• Before you begin, take time to look into the context of the book. Find out who wrote it and learn about the cultural climate it was written in, as well as where it fits on the biblical timeline. Then take time to read through the entire book of the Bible we are studying if you are able. This will help you to get the big picture of the book and will aid in comprehension, interpretation, and application.

• Start your study time with prayer. Ask God to help you understand what you are reading and allow it to transform you (Psalm 119:18).

• Look into the context of the book as well as the specific passage.

• Before reading what is written in the study, read the assigned passage! Repetitive reading is one of the best ways to study God's Word. Read it several times, if you are able, before going on to the study. Read in several translations if you find it helpful.

• As you read the text, mark down observations and questions. Write down things that stand out to you, things that you notice, or things that you don't understand. Look up important words in a dictionary or interlinear Bible.

• Look for things like verbs, commands, and references to God. Notice key terms and themes throughout the passage.

• After you have worked through the text, read what is written in the study. Take time to look up any cross-references mentioned as you study.

• Then work through the questions provided in the book. Read and answer them prayerfully.

• Paraphrase or summarize the passage, or even just one verse from the passage. Putting it into your own words helps you to slow down and think through every word.

• Focus your heart on the character of God that you have seen in this passage. What do you learn about God from the passage you have studied? Adore Him and praise Him for who He is.

• Think and pray through application and how this passage should change you. Get specific with yourself. Resist the urge to apply the passage to others. Do you have sin to confess? How should this passage impact your attitude toward people or circumstances? Does the passage command you to do something? Do you need to trust Him for something in your life? How does the truth of the gospel impact your everyday life?

• We recommend you have a Bible, pen, highlighters, and journal as you work through this study. We recommend that ballpoint pens instead of gel pens be used in the study book to prevent smearing. Here are several other optional resources that you may find helpful as you study:

• www.blueletterbible.org This free website is a great resource for digging deeper. You can find translation comparison, an interlinear option to look at words in the original languages, Bible dictionaries, and even commentary.

• A Dictionary. If looking up words in the Hebrew and Greek feels intimidating, look up words in English. Often times we assume we know the meaning of a word, but looking it up and seeing its definition can help us understand a passage better.

• A double-spaced copy of the text. You can use a website like www.biblegateway.com to copy the text of a passage and print out a double spaced copy to be able to mark on easily. Circle, underline, highlight, draw arrows, and mark in any way you would like to help you dig deeper and work through a passage.

The UPSIDE-DOWN KINGDOM

WEEK ONE // DAY ONE

MATTHEW 5-7

The Sermon on the Mount is Jesus' longest recorded sermon. It is also one of the most beautiful and well-known portions of Scripture. Much of its language has even crept into our pop culture as we often hear references from even non-believers to "turn the other cheek" or to follow "The Golden Rule." But the words of Jesus here are not just words; they are a manifesto of sorts for the kingdom of God. These words do not tell us how to become a Christian, but speak of how we should live because we as Christians have encountered the radical grace of God. Oswald Chambers said, "He came to make us what He teaches us we should be." And the truth is that these commands and principles are not things that we are capable of in our own strength. To live out the Sermon on the Mount, we are going to have to abide near the Vine (John 15). Martyn Lloyd-Jones reminds us that, "It not only states the demand; it points to the supply." This sermon doesn't just tell us how to live, but it points us to the Life-Giver Himself. It is on the pages of the Sermon on the Mount that we are pointed to Jesus.

The Sermon on the Mount is found in Matthew 5-7, as Matthew teaches the message of the kingdom of God. After the crowds had gathered around Jesus to hear Him teach and perform miracles, Jesus retreats to the mountain and begins to teach His disciples about the kingdom. The book of Matthew has echos of the story of Moses and the exodus from Egypt in its events and is presenting Jesus as the true and better Moses. It is no surprise then to see Jesus speaking from a mountain and giving the new rules for the kingdom, just as Moses heard God speak from Mount Sinai when the law was given. Jesus is coming to declare a new kingdom.

He sits down as a declaration of authority, just as He is now seated at the right hand of the Father, and speaks of the kingdom. This kingdom though is an upside-down kingdom. The Jews were on the lookout for the Messiah to come as a conquering king who would set up a political kingdom that would overthrow the Roman government that ruled over them. Instead, Jesus came. He came not to rule nations, but to rule the hearts of all those who would believe. This kingdom was different than what they expected. It was upside-down, and it was so much better than anything that they could have imagined.

The kingdom of God is the reign of God. The kingdom of God is now, and the kingdom of God is coming. It is already and not yet. He reigns now in our hearts, and some day, He will rule over every part of creation. The kingdom of God is in us, because He is in us. So Jesus proclaimed that the kingdom of God had arrived with Him (Matthew 4:17, 23), and He also preached a coming kingdom and even urged His disciples to pray for the kingdom of God to come (Matthew 6:10). Jesus was saying to those that listened that the kingdom of God that had been foretold in the Old Testament was here (Isaiah 52:7, Micah 5:7). He was saying that the Messiah that Israel had waited for to arrive was Him.

So the Sermon on the Mount is a description of what the life of a disciple of Jesus should look like. How should we live because of who He is and what He has done for us? Being a part of His kingdom should mean that we don't belong to the kingdom of this world. It means we see things differently, have different priorities, and live differently than this world. This is who Jesus wants His people to be. This isn't about a to-do list; it is about walking with the Spirit (Galatians 5:16, Ephesians 5:18). But He doesn't command us to do this in our own strength—He gives us Himself. He is our source of strength. He will do this in us. He is showing us who He is, and telling us what we should be, and then transforming us through His grace. This is the gospel.

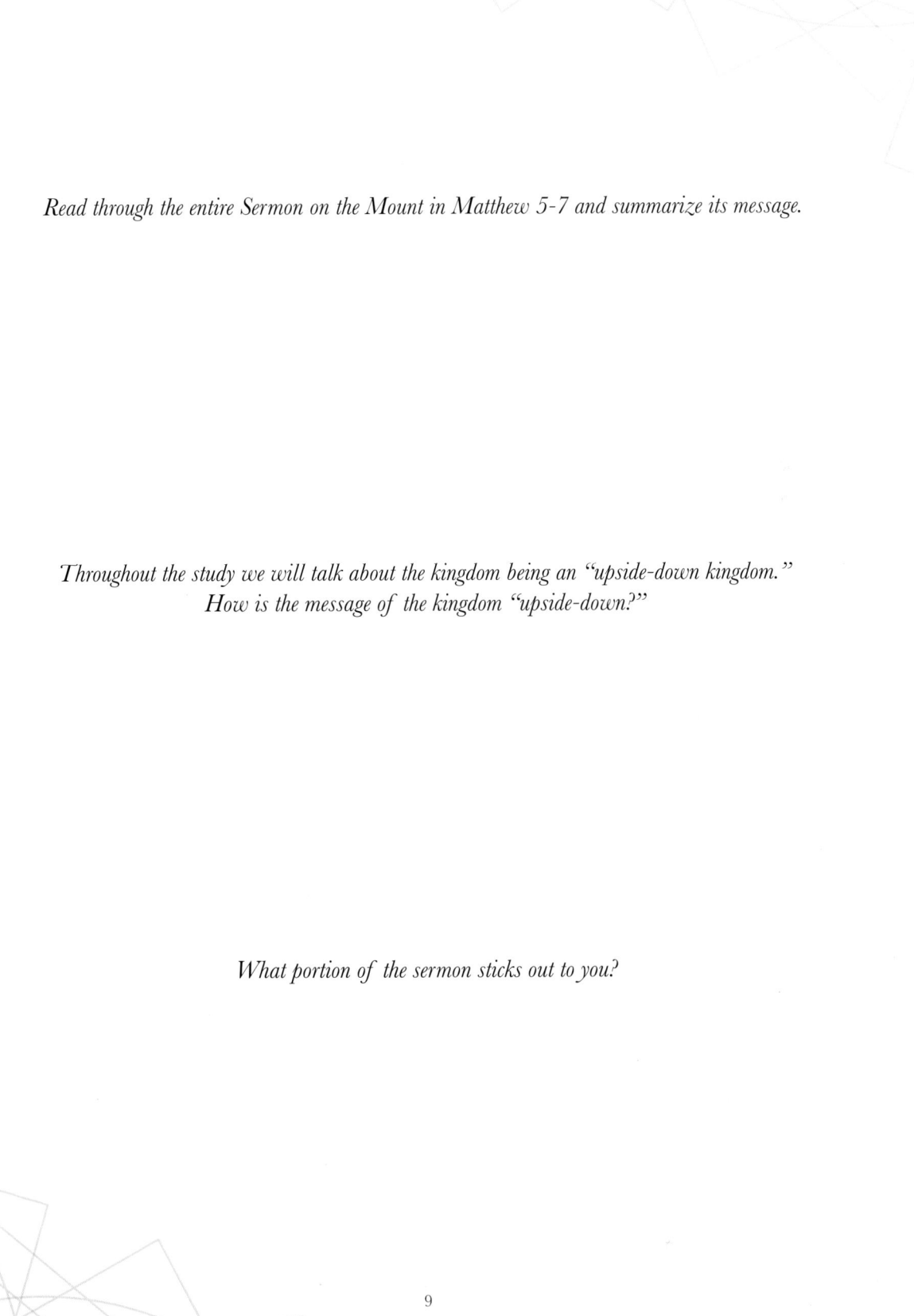

Read through the entire Sermon on the Mount in Matthew 5-7 and summarize its message.

Throughout the study we will talk about the kingdom being an "upside-down kingdom." How is the message of the kingdom "upside-down?"

What portion of the sermon sticks out to you?

MATTHEW 5:3

Jesus opened His mouth to speak this great sermon, and the first words that came from His lips were these, "Blessed are the poor in spirit, for theirs is the kingdom of heaven." The placement of these words at the very start of this sermon is no accident. These words are found at the start because this is the start of the Christian life. There is no Christian who has not found himself to be "poor in spirit." This is foundational to the gospel.

To be poor in spirit has nothing to do with being materially poor in this world, but instead this is a poverty of spirit. It is common for men to place their faith in riches. This happens to those that are both rich and poor. The rich put their confidence in wealth and want more wealth. The poor often seek after wealth in the same way, thinking that peace of mind and happiness would be found if only they had more. So Jesus is not speaking about poverty of finances, but poverty of spirit. To be poor in spirit means that we recognize our utter need before God. To be poor in spirit means that we see our desperate need for a Savior. It is in seeing our great need that we can see our great Savior. And it is when we are emptied of ourselves that we can be filled with Him.

This verse stands against the false notion that we can earn salvation or favor with God in our own strength. The gospel is this, that there is absolutely nothing we can do to earn His favor, that we are empty, broken, and poor, and that in ourselves we do not seek after God (Romans 3:10-18), and yet in His sovereign grace, He has sought after us and chosen us to be His children (Ephesians 1). He has taken us as poor beggars and made us sons and heirs (Galatians 4:1-7). Jesus who was rich made Himself poor, so that we could become rich in Him (2 Corinthians 8:9). Poverty of spirit is a mark of a person who understands the truth of the gospel. In ourselves we are the poorest beggars, yet in Him we are made the sons and daughters of God.

We come to Christ for salvation recognizing our poverty and need, and we should live day by day reminded of this great need. The world is going to tell you that "you are enough." But Scripture will remind us over and over again that we are not enough. We are not enough, but He is more than enough for us. Spurgeon said, "Our imaginary goodness is more difficult to conquer than our actual sin." How easy is it for us as believers to think we can live in our own strength, and yet Jesus is calling us to be poor in spirit and to lean into His strength—to be reminded that our hope is in Him and not in our performance.

Those who are poor in spirit are the people that have tasted the goodness of the gospel. We come to Jesus empty and leave full. This is the upside-down kingdom. It is the poor in spirit that possess the kingdom of God not just in the future, but right now. So we cultivate a heart that remembers who we are and what He has done for us. We look to Him as our source of strength and remember that we don't have to try to live in our own strength. As Robert Murray McCheyne said, "For every look at yourself, take ten looks at Christ. He is altogether lovely." We look to Jesus, and we keep looking. We look to Him in His Word as we search for His character, and we look to Him in prayer as we acknowledge our desperate need for Him. We look to Him as we remember where we were and what He has done. We look and we keep looking.

In what ways have you tried to live in your own strength? How do we live "poor in spirit?"

Paraphrase Matthew 5:3.

How can you look and keep looking to Christ?

MATTHEW 5:4

There is comfort for the grieved and mourning. Just as the beatitude to the poor in spirit was a spiritual lesson, so is this beatitude. "Those that mourn" here is not referring to those that mourn over death and loss, though there is certainly comfort from God for those things. This mourning goes even deeper. This mourning is the mourning over sin, over the fall, and over the state of the world. This is the result of a long hard look at our world and a long, hard look at ourselves—and yet the antidote to this grief is a look to our Savior because all comfort flows from Him.

Being someone that mourns does not mean that the Christian should never smile, or that they should be depressed about sin. It means that we should live in a holy tension of the reality of our fallen condition and of the bliss of redemption and the hope of restoration. The Puritan prayer book *The Valley of Vision* puts it this way,

"Grant me never to lose sight of
the exceeding sinfulness of sin,
the exceeding righteousness of salvation,
the exceeding glory of Christ,
the exceeding beauty of holiness,
the exceeding wonder of grace."

Living in this tension of mourning sin and the joy of grace is sorrow engulfed in hope. It is as we see our sin and we see our weakness that we are so aware of our need for Christ and for the grace and forgiveness that He offers. True joy in Christ is not possible if we have not first mourned over our sin and realized how deep our need was and how much Jesus has done for us.

We can look directly to Jesus for an example of someone who mourned over sin. Jesus did not mourn over personal sin because He is perfect, but He mourned over the sin of His people and He mourned over the effects of sin in this world. We see Him lamenting and weeping over Jerusalem (Matthew 23:37-39), and we see Him weeping over the impact of the fall and its effects on His people as He weeps at Lazarus' grave (John 11:28-44). He does not weep at Lazarus' grave out of desperation because He knew that He would raise him from the dead, instead He weeps at the impact that sin has caused on this world. He weeps because the people that He loves are weeping in loss because of life in a fallen world. The Old Testament tells us that Jesus was a man of sorrows, and it also tells us that He has carried our sorrow (Isaiah 53:3-4). The message of the Beatitudes has been compared to the prophecy of Jesus in Isaiah 61:1-3, and a glance at these verses shows us how the Messiah came to bind up the brokenhearted and comfort all who mourn. Jesus would make it clear in Luke 4:16-21 that He is the fulfillment of this passage. He is our Comforter. When we look at our sin and our weakness, we should mourn and grieve over it. When we look at what is happening in our world, we should be saddened and moved with compassion. But then we must shift our gaze to our God. We must look on His character and His attributes and be overwhelmed with the beauty of who He is. It is in Him that our comfort is found.

The mourning of our sin should make us rejoice in redemption and cling to the hope of restoration that is promised to believers (Revelation 21:4-6). As believers we should experience the grief of our sin at the moment of salvation, and then we should experience it over and over again as we wrestle with sin and grow in sanctification. We mourn, and we are instantly comforted. We look ahead to the glory that is to come and know with confidence that one day sin and sorrow will be gone (Romans 8:18). We look to Jesus who is the Comforter of our souls.

What sin in your life do you need to mourn over?

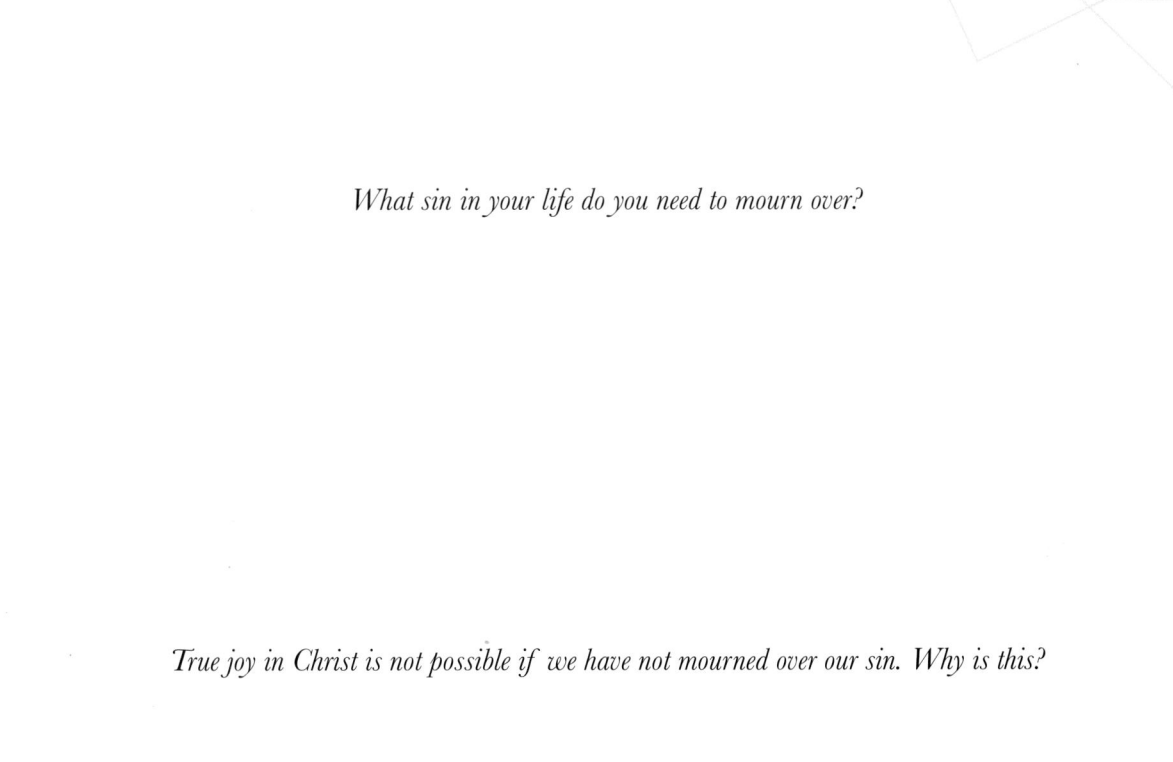

True joy in Christ is not possible if we have not mourned over our sin. Why is this?

How have you found comfort in God? How does your own sin and the state of this world make you long for the restoration that will come in heaven?

Blessed are THE MEEK, *for They Shall* INHERIT THE EARTH

WEEK ONE // DAY FOUR

MATTHEW 5:5

As we continue to look at the Beatitudes, we see that these descriptors of the blessed person build upon each other. As we approach verse 5, we see another descriptor of life in the upside-down kingdom. Here we see that "blessed are the meek, for they shall inherit the earth." This is not weakness but meekness that is being discussed. And meekness is strength under control. The Outline of Biblical Usage says this of meekness, "Meekness toward God is that disposition of spirit in which we accept His dealings with us as good, and therefore without disputing or resisting." Meekness definitely involves our attitude toward those around us, but most of all it is our heart attitude toward our God.

The Greek word her for "meek" is only used a total of four times in the New Testament. It is used here in the Beatitudes, twice to describe Jesus (Matthew 11:28-29, Matthew 21:5), and once to describe a woman of virtue (1 Peter 3:4). This is the character of Jesus that we should be taking on as believers. This is the opposite of self-sufficiency, self-righteousness, and pride. This is the heart attitude of a person toward the Lord, no matter what situation they find themselves in. This is joy in every circumstance. This is not shallow happiness, but deep and enduring joy despite the situations of life. In heaven, we will be able to look back at our lives and see that God was working everything for our good (Romans 8:28), and we will be able to say that God had showed us "only goodness and mercy" (Psalm 23:6), but the meek person tastes a glimpse of that attitude here on earth. It is not simply words that are said, or a "#blessed" tagged at the end of a social media post. It is confidence and hope when things look bad. It is hope when the situation seems hopeless. It is faith and confidence that God will keep His promises and that He will be faithful.

This meekness is a form of submission and humility. Submission to God's ultimate and unwavering sovereignty and the humility to recognize that He knows what is best. It is also contentment—contentment that pours out in every situation (Philippians 4:11-13). It is a contentment that knows that we don't have to have all the things of this life to have what really matters. It is a contentment whether rich or poor that there is nothing that compares to Jesus. In Him we have everything (2 Corinthians 6:13).

And in the upside-down kingdom that Jesus preached, it is the meek that inherit the earth. It is the ones that have humbled themselves before God and are aware of their utter need that are co-heirs with Christ of the whole earth (Romans 8:17, Galatians 4:6-7). It is the meek that have it all just because they have Him. Jesus Himself is our example of meekness. He did not come as a warrior king like the people expected the Messiah to come. He did not come to conquer the powers of Rome but to conquer the hearts of His people. Passages like Philippians 2:3-11 and Matthew 11:28-29 show us who Jesus is and who we should be. He is humble and meek, and Philippians 2 reminds us that we are called to be like Him by telling us to have this mind among us. We are to think like Him. We are to live like Him.

This meekness is an outworking of a heart that is surrendered to the Lord and to His will above all. It is the natural step for one that is poor in spirit and mourns their sinful state to be meek before God and man. Sinclair Ferguson said, "When we know what we are before God, and look to Him for grace and salvation, then we become poor in spirit; then we mourn for our sins; having seen ourselves as we really are, we bow to his will in all things. And as we experience the gentleness of grace, we are meek and gentle with others." This should be the impact of the gospel. The gospel was never meant to be something that is needed only at the time of conversion. We need the gospel each day to point us back to our fallen state and to His magnificent grace. The gospel is meant to transform us. It is His grace that saves us from sin and clothes us in the righteousness of God, and it is the gospel that sanctifies us day by day and transforms us into the image of Jesus. May our prayer be that we will be transformed into a person that is meek—a person that submits and surrenders to our God, a person that pours out grace for others in the same way that it has been poured out for us.

How is meekness the next step in the progression after poverty of spirit and mourning for sin?

Our society is not a big fan of meekness, and yet this is how Jesus is described. Look up Philippians 2:3-11 and Matthew 11:28-29 and record observations about the character of Jesus.

How can meekness be cultivated in your life? What situations do you need to place in the hands of God? What people do you need to respond to with grace and humility?

Blessed are Those WHO HUNGER *and Thirst for* RIGHTEOUSNESS, *for They Shall* BE SATISFIED

WEEK ONE // DAY FIVE

MATTHEW 5:6

This fourth beatitude shows a shift in the passage. And this beatitude in so many ways sums up the entire Christian life. This should be what we live for. We should be people with a hunger and a thirst for righteousness. This beatitude is a culmination of the ones that have come before. Sinclair Ferguson says, "For once we have discovered that we have no resources to save ourselves, we learn to look elsewhere – to Christ – to meet our needs, and also to meet the needs of the world in which we live." As we recognize our spiritual poverty, and as we mourn over our sin, and surrender to God's sovereign ways, we can then come to the place where we hunger and thirst after righteousness.

Righteousness is the center of this verse, and it is a theme throughout the Sermon on the Mount. The word "righteousness" has two facets. In one sense, this is justification. This is the imputed righteousness of God to us when we accept God's grace for salvation. In salvation, we are not just forgiven of our sin, but we are given the righteousness of Jesus. He takes our sin and gives us His righteousness (2 Corinthians 5:21). Jesus Himself is our righteousness. We could not be righteous on our own, but He is our righteousness and this righteousness is received by faith in His grace (1 Corinthians 1:30, Philippians 3:9). Righteousness is our justification or right relationship with God, but it is also our sanctification. As believers, we possess the imputed righteousness of God, and yet we also are in a process of sanctification in which we are constantly becoming more like Jesus. We are constantly growing in Him and becoming more like Him. We already have His righteousness, and yet we are putting on His righteousness as we allow Him to transform us and grow us in holiness. 2 Corinthians 3:18 describes us being transformed from one degree of glory to another. We are slowly glimpsing who He is and being transformed by His character.

The words "hunger" and "thirst" in the verse are used to describe the fervent and diligent longing for God's righteousness. The words remind us of Psalm 42 that tells us that our souls should long for God as the deer pants for the water. We should hunger and thirst to be the holy people that God desires for us to be. He changes our desires. Though we once longed for the things of this world, the more we abide in Him, the more we hunger and thirst for Him above all else. This is a longing to be holy. This is a desire to walk with God that is stronger than any other desire in our hearts. This is a desire for the restoration of creation and a desire for God's kingdom to come on earth—a desire for the nations to be reached, for social justice to reign, and for our own sinful hearts to be transformed in the light of His glory.

Only the hungry can be satisfied. And there is no satisfaction apart from Him. Blessedness comes only through righteousness, and righteousness comes only through Him. This is the already, but not yet of our faith. We have this righteousness at the moment of salvation, and yet we are also growing in righteousness and yearning for it. We do not seek after happiness or blessedness; we seek after Jesus and His righteousness, happiness, and blessedness are poured out on those that hunger and thirst for who He is. *Only Jesus satisfies.*

So we must allow Him to cultivate in our hearts a hunger and a thirst for righteousness. We must abide in Him and realize that we can't do it on our own (John 15). We must realize that there is no satisfaction apart from Him. He is the one that we long for. To walk with God is what our hearts yearn for and what our souls hunger and thirst for. And when we surrender to Him, and hunger and thirst for righteousness, He promises that we *will* be satisfied.

What things do people hunger and thirst after that they think will bring satisfaction?

Paraphrase Matthew 5:6.

How can you cultivate in your heart and life a hunger and thirst for righteousness?

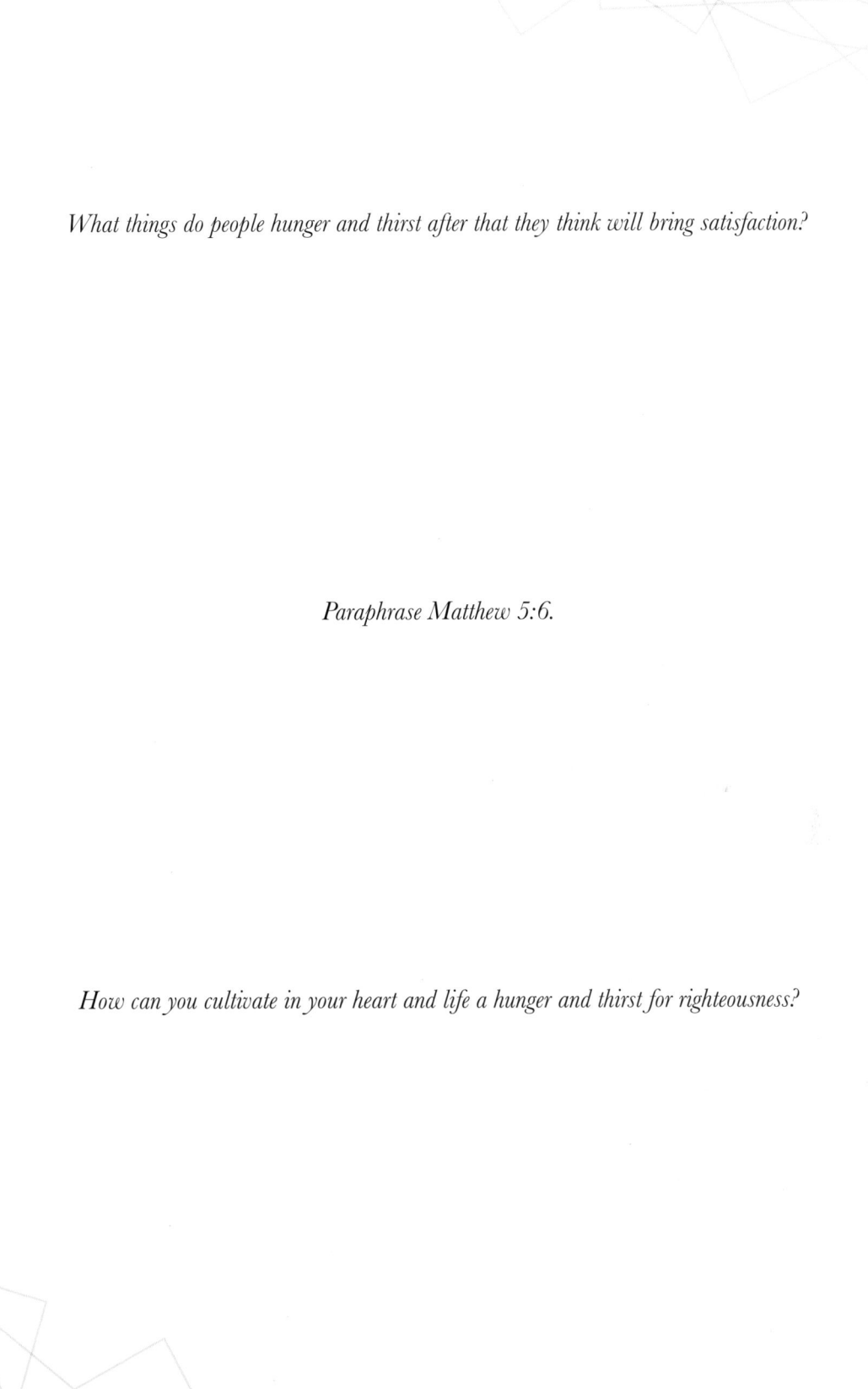

Blessed are those who hunger and thirst for righteousness, for they will be filled.

MATTHEW 5:6

WEEKLY REFLECTION

WEEK ONE

Read Matthew 5:1-6

▸▸ *Paraphrase the passage from this week.*

▸▸ *What did you observe from this week's text about God and His character?*

▸▸ *What does the passage teach about the condition of mankind and about yourself?*

▶▶ *How does this passage point to the gospel?*

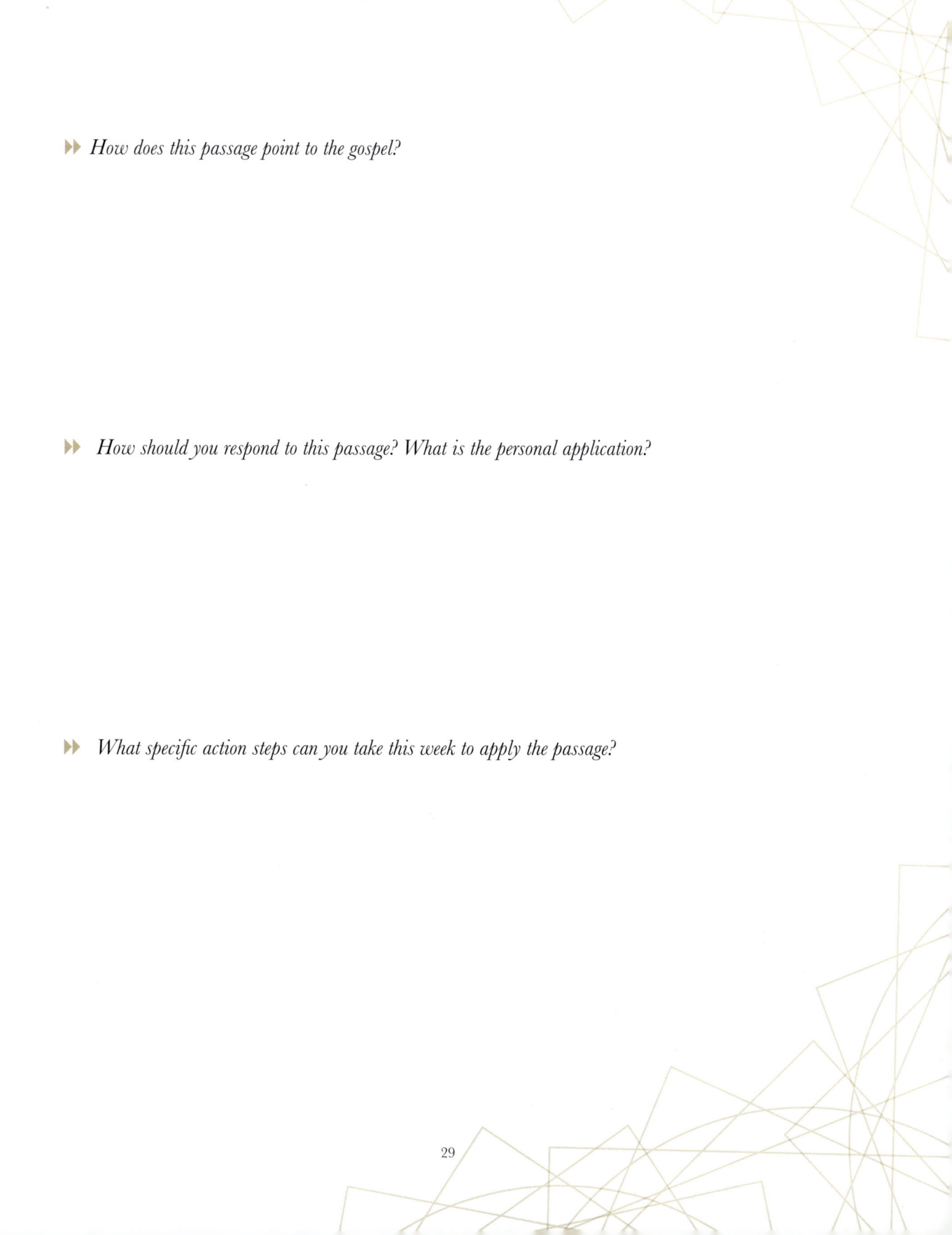

▶▶ *How should you respond to this passage? What is the personal application?*

▶▶ *What specific action steps can you take this week to apply the passage?*

MATTHEW 5:7

The Beatitudes make us take a long, hard look at ourselves, and yet they also turn our gaze to Jesus who perfectly fulfills each beatitude. As we look at this description of what a believer should be, we are reminded that we fall short each day, and yet Jesus is our perfect example. He is the one that we look to who perfectly demonstrates every character trait of this grand sermon.

It is so important for us to remember as we study this sermon, and specifically the Beatitudes, that these are not isolated statements. These must be read in their context and the whole sermon taken together. Each phrase and each beatitude builds upon each other. This is about the sum total of the character of the believer which is a reflection of the character of Jesus Himself. Martyn-Lloyd Jones said, "The Christian gospel places all its primary emphasis upon being, rather than doing. The gospel puts greater weight upon our attitude than upon our actions…we have to *be* Christian before we can act as Christians." Truly, the Christian life is about being and not just doing. It is about transformation (Romans 12:2, 2 Corinthians 3:18, Philippians 3:10). It is about being born again (John 3:3, 1 Peter 1:3, 23). It is about new life (Ephesians 4:24, Colossians 3:10). It is about being a new creation (2 Corinthians 5:17). In essence, the Beatitudes are telling us to be who we are. We are in Christ, and now we are called to be like Him.

The Beatitudes in many ways mimic the Ten Commandments. Here we see, just as in the Ten Commandments, a shift from the relationship between God and man to the relationship between man and fellow man. Our relationship with God impacts our relationship with others and that is clearly seen in this beatitude. Many have gotten hung up on this beatitude and have wondered if it is teaching that God will not have mercy on us in salvation if we are not merciful people. This is totally against the truth of the gospel that we are saved by His grace and mercy. There is nothing that we can do to earn our salvation. Instead, Jesus is saying that we should show mercy to others because we have received mercy. We do not earn mercy, but showing mercy to others is an evidence that we have received mercy and that we understand the mercy that we have been given. If we do not extend mercy, we do not understand the mercy that has been poured out on us.

Mercy is a huge theme in Scripture. God's desire for His people to show mercy is seen throughout the Old Testament (Hosea 6:6, Micah 6:8, Proverbs 21:13). In the New Testament, mercy is personified in none other than Jesus Himself who is our ultimate example of mercy. In Matthew 12:20, we see that Jesus is the fulfillment of the prophecy spoken by Isaiah in Isaiah 42:3 that He would not break a bruised reed, or quench a wick that was about to burn out. Jesus did not come to hurt the hurting, but to bring healing. He will mend the broken and carefully care for them. He will put kindling around the fire that is about to go out and bring it back to life. This is what Jesus does for us. It is the same Jesus who cries out for the Father to forgive those that are brutally killing Him (Luke 23:34). It is the same Jesus who extends mercy to sinners, and showers them in His grace, not because of anything that we can do, but because He loved us.

Mercy isn't something that comes naturally to us. It is only Jesus working in us and transforming us to be more like Him that can make us merciful. It is as these beatitudes build and build upon each other that our character is transformed from one that seeks to please self to one that is like Him. It is as we recognize our spiritual poverty and our deep need that we can be merciful to others in the same condition. It is as we mourn for our sin, and recognize who we are without God, that we can extend mercy to others in their sin. It is as we are meek and seek after God's will and not our own that we can extend mercy. It is when we truly come to a place where we hunger and thirst for righteousness that we can extend mercy. It is when we realize that our satisfaction comes from God alone that we can be merciful. It is then that we can stop worrying about our own desires and desire Him alone.

How is Jesus the perfect picture of mercy?

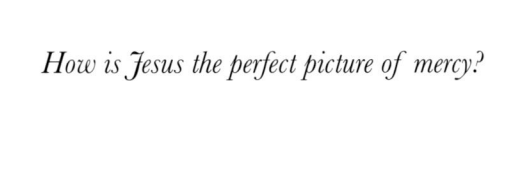

Why should we show mercy to other people?

*Think about a person in your life that you need to intentionally extend mercy to.
Write out a prayer asking God to help you be merciful.*

MATTHEW 5:8

These precious words of Jesus just keep building upon each other. Our hearts cannot help but see our utter need and the extravagant beauty of the gospel. Jesus speaks in this beatitude about being pure of heart. This isn't about outward conformity or about other people thinking that we are good. It is about a transformed heart. This kind of heart transformation is not possible on our own. No matter how hard we try, we cannot do this on our own. That may feel like bad news, but in fact it is the very best news there ever was. We can't do it on our own, but He can do it for us. In Ezekiel 36:25-26, a new covenant was promised. We are given a new heart. We are given His Spirit within us. This heart only comes from God. We must be born again to receive the new heart that He offers (John 3:7). There is nothing that we can do on our own; it is simply a gift of His grace accepted by faith (Ephesians 2:8-9). In so many ways, we must be poor before our hearts can be pure. We must have the poverty of spirit spoken of in Matthew 5:3 before we can ever have a pure heart. We must also mourn over our sin. We must mourn over the uncleanness in ourselves before we can rejoice over the new heart that comes only from the Lord.

But having a pure heart is also about having a heart that is unwaveringly committed to the Lord alone. It is about having a single focus. It is about serving the Lord, not out of a sense of duty or for personal gain, but out of complete dedication and love to Him. It isn't just about doing the right things—it is about doing the right things as a result of a pure heart overflowing with love and gratitude for our God. It isn't about pure actions, but a pure heart. If it is important for us to have a single focus, then we must ask ourselves, "what is my single focus?" What is the thing that you desire above all else?

The heart here is not just our emotions. The Outline of Biblical Usage defines it this way, "It is the fountain and seat of the thoughts, passions, desires, appetites, affections, purposes, endeavors." *Our heart is who we are*. It is our mind and our emotions. When everything else is stripped away, it is the longing of our soul. If we want our hearts to beat for our God and for the gospel, we are probably going to have to strip some things away. We are going to have to recognize that Jesus is not only the best thing, He is the *only* thing. Sinclair Ferguson put it this way, "Great things can be completely obscured by small things if the small things are brought near enough to our eyes…We see that this world has nothing to compare to Jesus Christ and all that he offers to us. But when we hold this world and its contents too near, we no longer see Christ and His glory so clearly." May we never hold this world so closely that we can't see the most important One. May we set our hearts and minds on the things above, the things that really matter, the things that last for eternity, and not settle for the lesser things of this world (Colossians 3:2). Let's set our hearts on Him.

And the result of us having let Him work in us, of giving us a new heart, and of giving us a heart that is pure with one single focus, is that we will see God. We will see Him in this world. We will see Him in our circumstances. We will see Him in His Word. We will know Him. Our whole perception will be changed. A sunrise is a gift of common grace that is available to all men, and yet when we grasp the truth that the God of the universe has carefully crafted the majesty of the sunset, and yet also called us by name, we will see it in a whole new way. We will see His sovereign hand in every circumstance of our life. It may not be clear to the world around, but to the one who is so near to Him, His hand will be evident in every situation. We will open His Word with passionate hearts and seek to see Him on every page. We will know Him. We will know who He is. We will love what He loves and hate what He hates. And we will look forward with eager and expectant hearts to the day when we see Him face to face (1 Corinthians 13:12). We will long for the day when we will see with our eyes the One that we now see with our hearts.

How do the other beatitudes build up to this one?

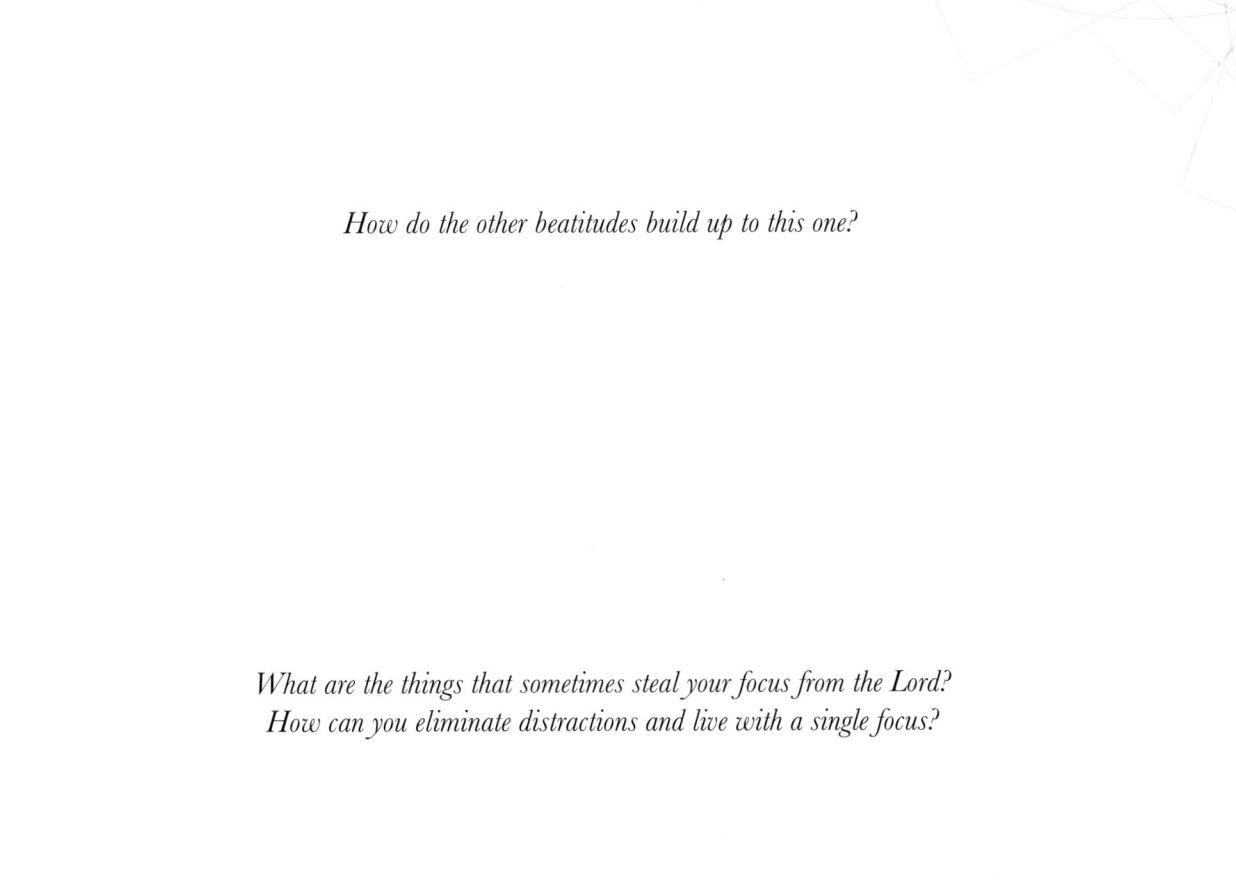

*What are the things that sometimes steal your focus from the Lord?
How can you eliminate distractions and live with a single focus?*

How do you think having a pure heart enables us to see God?

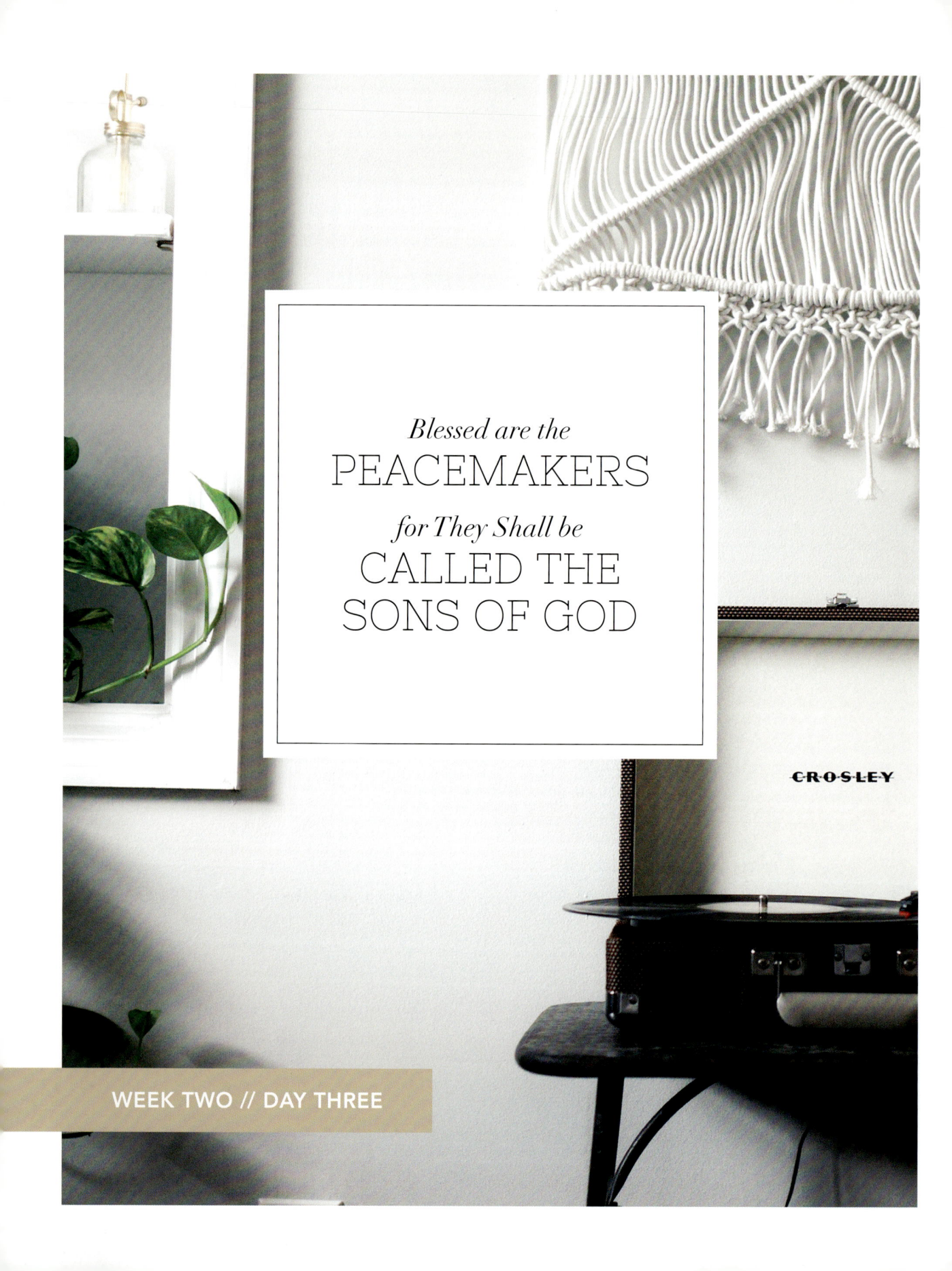

Blessed are the
PEACEMAKERS
for They Shall be
CALLED THE SONS OF GOD

WEEK TWO // DAY THREE

MATTHEW 5:9

Our God is a God of peace. So the call for us to be peacemakers is a call for us to be transformed into His image. As people created in the image of God, or the imago dei, we are to reflect this aspect of God's character. Yet the fall and curse have revealed our sinful nature. So often we would rather stand up for our own rights than lay down ourselves to bring peace. But through the power of God, we as His children can once again be peacemakers as we are transformed into His likeness. These words must have struck the disciples. Throughout the Gospels, we see the disciples confused about what the ministry of the Messiah would be. They wanted a warrior king who would conquer the political powers of the day and overturn all that was wrong in the political system, and instead Jesus came as a humble servant with a message of peace. But the peace that Jesus was preaching wasn't just about being passive or not standing up for truth. This was peace between man and God. Jesus was coming to preach about *shalom* peace. Peace that brought wholeness and completeness that had been destroyed by the fall.

This should be a characteristic of every believer. This isn't about personality in the same way that we have seen with the other beatitudes. These are not characteristics that flow out of our natural dispositions. These are fruits that are only brought about by the Spirit inside us as believers. We have no strength to muster them up on our own. It is interesting to notice the placement of this beatitude as it falls right after the message about being pure in heart. James 3:17-18 puts these fruits in this same order as it tells us that God's wisdom is first pure and then peaceable among so many other things. We cannot be peacemakers if we do not have a heart that has been made pure by God.

Being a peacemaker is not about passivity. This is about a fervent desire for all to find shalom peace with God. And though peace with the church and peace with other people is a part of being a peacemaker, a peacemaker is first and foremost an evangelist. A peacemaker is someone that desires for all to find the shalom peace with God. The message of peace is the message of the gospel. Jesus brought peace to us through the cross (Colossians 1:20), and Ephesians 2:14 tells us that He Himself is our peace. He has broken down every division between people and made us one people in Him. When we have peace with God, we can have peace with other people because God's peace is ruling in our hearts (Colossians 3:15).

Being a peacemaker does not mean that life will be easy. It does not mean that there will be no conflict. It means that with everything you are you will choose to lay down your own preferences and point others to the One who gives peace. Martyn Lloyd Jones said, "The peacemaker has only one concern, and it is the glory of God amongst men." May we have a pure heart that is concerned with being a peacemaker. Being a peacemaker is not about appeasing the crowds or ensuring that there is never conflict. It is about addressing our own sinful hearts and hiding them in Christ. It is about realizing that the great need of man is not conformation to religion but transformation by the Savior. It is seeing that God alone can turn hearts that were once selfish and wicked and make them into hearts that seek after the glory of God alone and the furtherance of the gospel message. May we focus our hearts on being who we have been made to be instead of doing the things that we think that we should do. May we gaze on the Prince of Peace and become people of peace. We are His children and we will be called the sons of God. May we draw near to the Son who has brought peace through the cross (Colossians 1:20), so that we can bring His message of peace to this world.

Being a peacemaker is being like Jesus.

What does it look like to live as a peacemaker?

How can you live in a way that draws others to the Lord?

How is being a peacemaker ultimately more about who we are than about what we do?

Blessed are Those Who are
PERSECUTED
for Righteousness'
SAKE,
for Theirs is
THE KINGDOM OF HEAVEN

WEEK TWO // DAY FOUR

MATTHEW 5:10-12

The beatitudes end with the bookended promise the same as the first Beatitude—the promise that this person possesses the kingdom of heaven. But the final beatitude is another example of the upside-down kingdom. You would think that after all of the time that we have spent studying this sermon already that we would have become accustomed to the upside-down message of the gospel. Yet it is so difficult for us to wrap our finite human minds around these heavenly truths. We find in this final beatitude that there is blessing for the one who is persecuted for the sake of righteousness. This is a blessing for those who are persecuted for Jesus who is the righteous One. In our minds we would think that if a person possesses all the characteristics set forth in the Beatitudes that the world would love that person, and yet the final beatitude tells us that those people that are poor in spirit, mourn for sin, are meek, hunger and thirst for righteousness, are merciful, pure in heart, and peacemakers, are the very people that will be persecuted by this world.

We serve a Savior who was persecuted, and we serve a Savior who was crucified, so this persecution should not come as a shock to us. Even now, the One who came to bring life abundant to this world is reviled and spoken ill of. Jesus Himself reminded the disciples in John 15:18-20 that the world would hate them just as it hated Him. This same evil world will hate us as well. Being a disciple of Jesus and possessing genuine holiness creates tension with the world around, and even with so-called nominal Christians who claim to be children of God, but stand in opposition to the things that Jesus taught. The life of righteousness and blessedness is offensive to them because the gospel itself is offensive (1 Corinthians 1:18). So often in Scripture we see persecution coming from the religious. It comes from those who claim religion and keep up with the religious status quo, but never allow the truth of the gospel to transform their hearts. We must proclaim the true gospel and the God of the gospel with both our words and with our lives.

We must be careful though as we read this final beatitude that we notice that Jesus is speaking of those who are persecuted for righteousness' sake and on His account. We cannot be critical and harsh and then claim that we are being persecuted in His name. This beatitude is not an excuse for us to sin in His name. This is speaking of those persecuted for righteousness sake, and not of those being persecuted because they are self-righteous. We must guard our hearts against the notion that we are better than others. We possess the same depraved nature, and it is only by God's grace that we have been made new. It is nothing of ourselves (Ephesians 2:8-9).

And what is our response if we are persecuted in His name? Should it be to complain, to pout, to slander the evil, or to leave nasty comments on social media? No. Our response to being persecuted as Jesus would tell us is to rejoice and be glad. It seems again like such an upside-down response to being wronged. Yet when we are fully convinced that this world is not our home, it becomes so much easier to do. When we recognize that we live for another kingdom, we can endure suffering for Him just as He endured suffering for us.

The interesting thing about this beatitude is that Jesus turned it to the disciples and changed the tense in which He was speaking beginning in verse 11. He made it personal for them, and we can be sure that He is making it personal for us. Jesus is looking at His disciples (and He has called us to be disciples as well), and He is telling them that there is a kingdom far beyond any kingdom on earth. And in this kingdom, the poor in spirit possess the kingdom, those who mourn are comforted, the meek inherit the earth, those that hunger and thirst for righteousness are satisfied, the merciful receive mercy, the pure in heart see their God, the peacemakers are called His children, and those that are persecuted in His name are given the keys to the kingdom. This is the description of God's people. This is who we are and this is who He is making us to be.

By His grace.

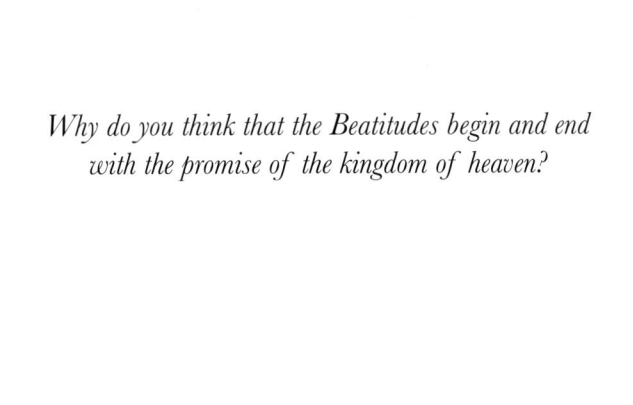

*Why do you think that the Beatitudes begin and end
with the promise of the kingdom of heaven?*

Why does the gospel push against the world and those with an empty religion?

Which beatitude stuck out most to you and why?

The
SALT
of the
EARTH

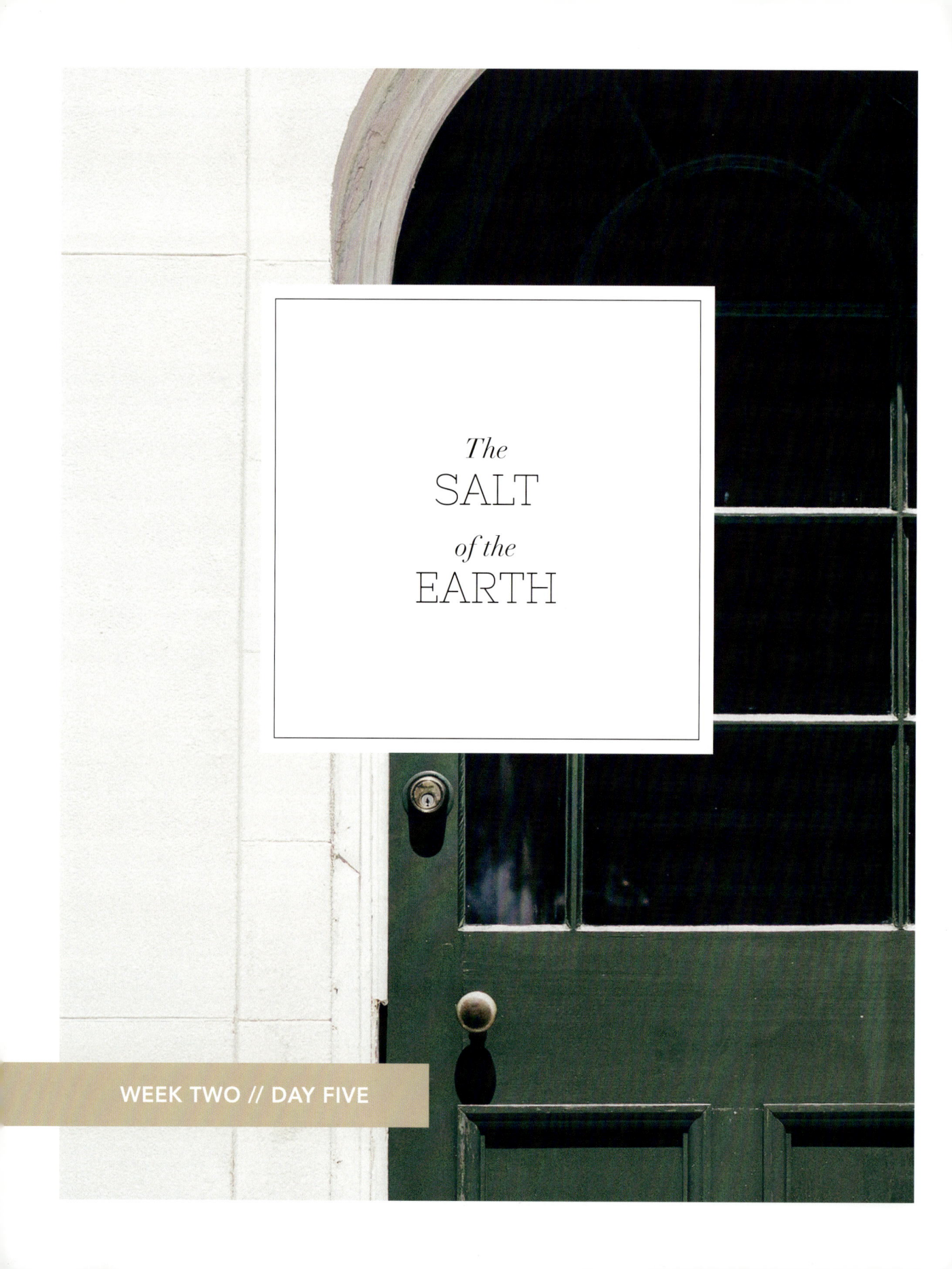

WEEK TWO // DAY FIVE

MATTHEW 5:13

In the Beatitudes, Jesus told the disciples, and us, who we are as disciples of Jesus in this upside-down kingdom. Now, as the Sermon on the Mount continues, Jesus will explain how disciples should influence the world around them. There is a very similar construction in 1 Peter 2:9-12 as believers are named as a chosen people, royal priesthood, etc, and then told how they should live in light of who they are. The same thing is happening in these verses. Jesus has declared not just what we should strive to be, but He has told us about our kingdom identity as His disciples. Now He will begin to tell us how who we are should impact how we live and those around us. The kingdom had come in its "already" form with the advent of Jesus, and all believers await the "not yet" that will occur when He returns at the second advent. Jesus is answering the question, "What does it mean to live as a disciple?" Sinclair Ferguson explains it this way, "What did Jesus mean when he said that Christians are salt? Notice that he said, 'You are the salt of the earth.' The mood of the verb is indicative (a statement of fact), not imperative (command to be something). Jesus is not urging his disciples to become something that they are not; he is telling them what they are as kingdom people." As followers of Jesus, we are being called to walk in the identity that we have already been given. We are to be who He has made us to be.

So what is the purpose of salt? How are we to live lives that fulfill what He has made us to be? Salt does several different things. The first thing salt does is to *preserve*. Salt preserves things from decay, and in the same way our lives as believers are meant to shine into the world around us. This does not mean that our lives have the power to bring lasting change to the world. *Only Jesus can do that.* But this world gets a glimpse of who Jesus is through our lives. You may have seen this use in your own life or in the life of someone you know. Have you ever noticed how those that know that you are a Christ-follower act a little differently when you are around? Perhaps they don't curse, or perhaps they don't talk about the same things they would if you were not there. This is what salt does. Salt keeps at bay the effects of decay and encourages those around it to live in an upright manner.

Salt also *seasons*. Salt added to food will bring out the flavor of the dish. As believers who are called to be salt, we should be bringing out what is inside us to the world around us. And what is in us is Jesus. We should demonstrate to the world around us what it means to live the abundant life that Jesus has given to us (John 10:10). We should possess deep and abiding joy that is not dependent on our circumstances. We should possess such a peace that the world longs to know the cause or the hope that is within us.

Salt also makes us *thirst*. A salty meal will make us crave water. In the same way, the saltiness of the life of the believer should make other people crave the Living Water (John 4, 6:35). Our lives should make people thirsty for Jesus. As they see what Jesus is to us, it should give them a deep longing to drink of the water of life that He so freely offers to all.

Salt makes a difference. It seems that Jesus was not as pessimistic as so many believers today who have given up on reaching out to the world around us and have concluded that things have just gotten too bad. *No*. Jesus commanded us to go and make disciples, and He commanded us to do that by others seeing the goodness of God through a transformed life. Yet the verse ends with an admonition for us to not lose the saltiness that we have been given. In the first century culture, salt would not be refined and could easily be contaminated if it mixed with other things. If the salt was mixed with dust, it would not have the impact that pure salt would have. So Jesus points us to this truth and encourages us to live pure lives. We must do what Paul commanded the Colossians to do in Colossians 3:5 and put to death the sin that so easily can weigh us down and cause us to lose our saltiness. We must stay near Jesus so that we can fulfill our purpose and influence the world around us as we point them to Jesus alone.

How does the world get a glimpse of Jesus through us?

How can your life make people thirsty for the things of God?

What are some practical things you can do this week to live out your calling to be the salt of the earth?

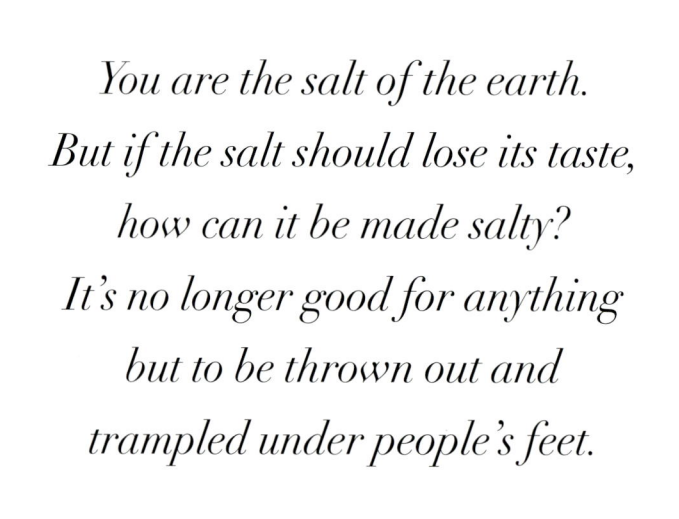

*You are the salt of the earth.
But if the salt should lose its taste,
how can it be made salty?
It's no longer good for anything
but to be thrown out and
trampled under people's feet.*

MATTHEW 5:13

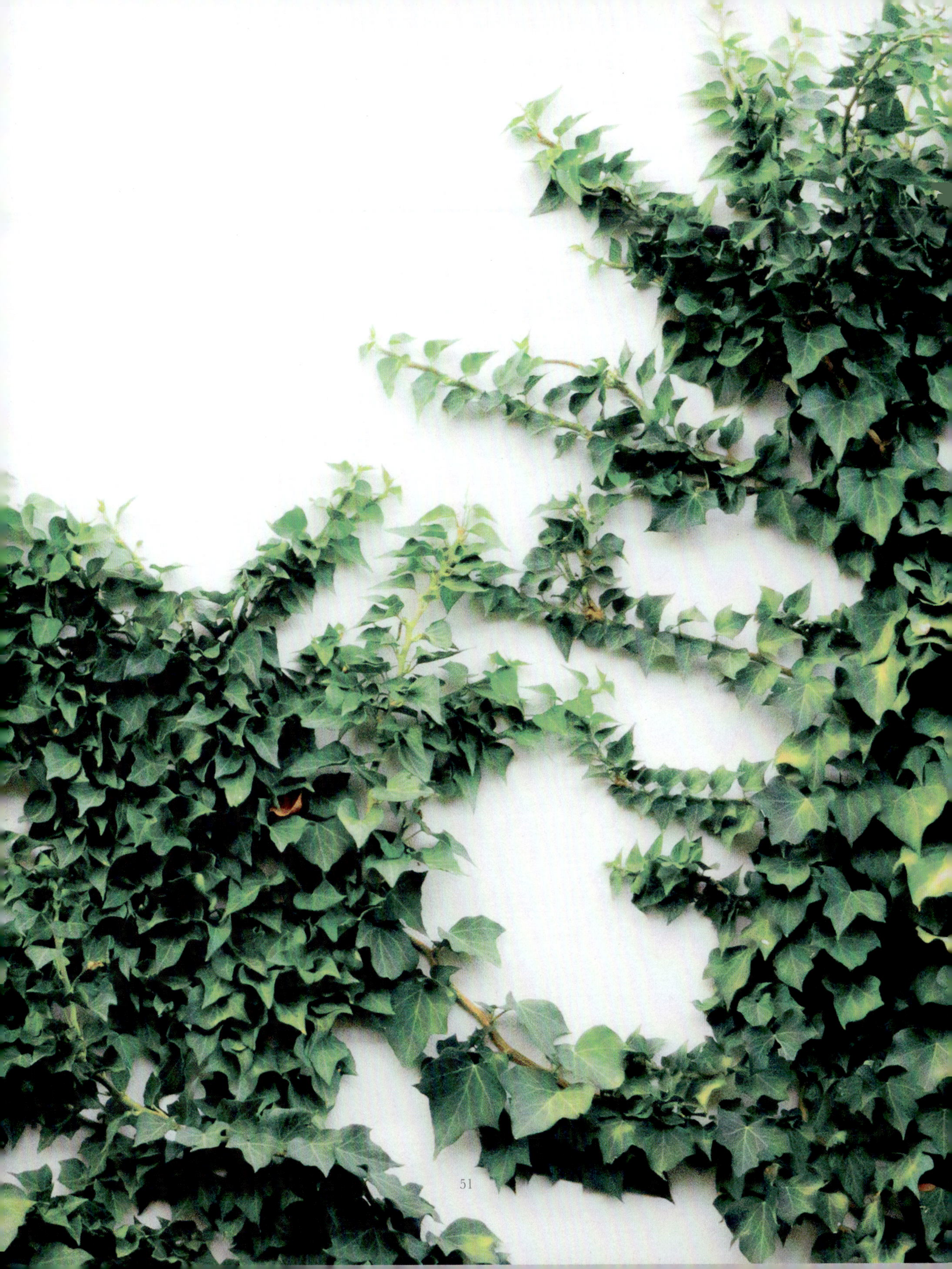

WEEKLY REFLECTION

WEEK TWO

Read Matthew 5:7-13

▶▶ *Paraphrase the passage from this week.*

▶▶ *What did you observe from this week's text about God and His character?*

▶▶ *What does the passage teach about the condition of mankind and about yourself?*

▶▶ *How does this passage point to the gospel?*

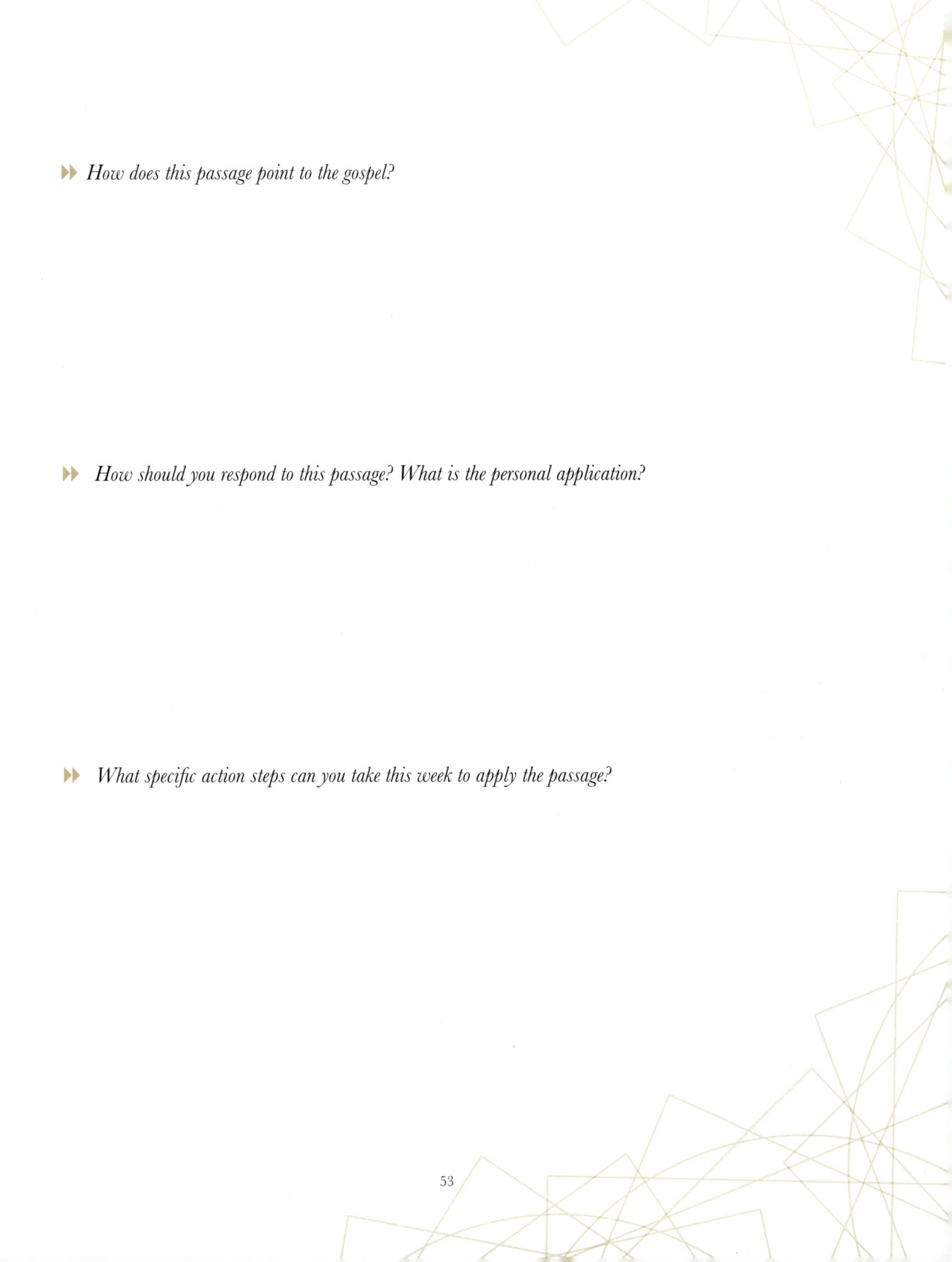

▶▶ *How should you respond to this passage? What is the personal application?*

▶▶ *What specific action steps can you take this week to apply the passage?*

This
LITTLE LIGHT
of
MINE

WEEK THREE // DAY ONE

MATTHEW 5:14-16

As disciples of Jesus, we are called to be the light of the world. We cannot go too far into thinking through what it means to be the light of the world, without first recognizing that Jesus Himself is the Light of the World (John 8:12). So as we are called to be the light of the world, we are being called to be like Jesus—to follow in His footsteps as we shine His light to the world around us. Again, we are being called to be who He has already made us to be as His followers. The imagery of light and darkness is seen all over Scripture. Some verses remind us that as believers, we have been brought out of the kingdom of darkness (Colossians 1:12-14), and other verses urge us to walk as children of light (Ephesians 5:8-14). We are called to reflect His light.

It can be hard for us to fully understand the far reach of darkness in the first century world. We live with the modern convenience of electricity, and we don't know too much of total darkness. This city set on a hill would be visible for miles around by shining light into the darkness of the countryside. In the same way, as Christians, the light of Jesus should shine forth from us into the pitch black darkness of this world around us. Jesus also says that our light should not be hidden under a bushel. The words quickly bring to mind the children's song,"This Little Light of Mine." We are not to hide our lights under a bushel; we are to let them shine. There are so many things that can cause our light to be hidden. John Stott said, "You are light, and so you must let your light shine and not conceal it in any way, whether by sin or by compromise, by laziness or by fear." For each of us it will be different. We will be tempted to hide our light instead of letting it shine forth for Him. We will be tempted to worry more about our own pride or reputation than about His. We will be tempted to live in the sin that we are supposed to expose. We will be tempted to think that the darkness is not that bad. We will be tempted to let our own fear keep us from shining as light for Him. We may be tempted to hide from the darkness of the world, but with God's strength we can shine light into that darkness. We can allow darkness to discourage us, or we can allow it to compel us even more to do what God has called us to do. The purpose of light is to shine, and we were created to shine as lights for God.

Light exposes darkness. It makes things visible. Light shows us what we could not see before. Light guides as we navigate this world. Light causes things to grow. Jesus is the light, and we are to reflect His light to the world around us. We are going to have to be different than the world to shine into it. We are going to need to get near Jesus so that His light can shine in and through us to the world around us. We must be disciples of Jesus and not disciples of this world.

In all these things, our goal is for His glory and not our own. We shine our lights never to point to ourselves but always to point to Him. The purpose of shining as a light is so that others will see God in us and will give glory to Him alone (1 Peter 2:12). Martyn Lloyd-Jones said, "We are only 'the light of the world' as He who is 'the light of the world' works in and through us." We cannot be the light of the world in our own strength. It must be Him working in us to shine into the darkness of the world around us. And the goal is never to show how great we are or to point to ourselves. The goal is to point to the One who is in us—the One who has taken our weakness to show His strength and has transformed us from children of darkness to children of light. Our testimony is a light to those around us, because Jesus is the light that is within us.

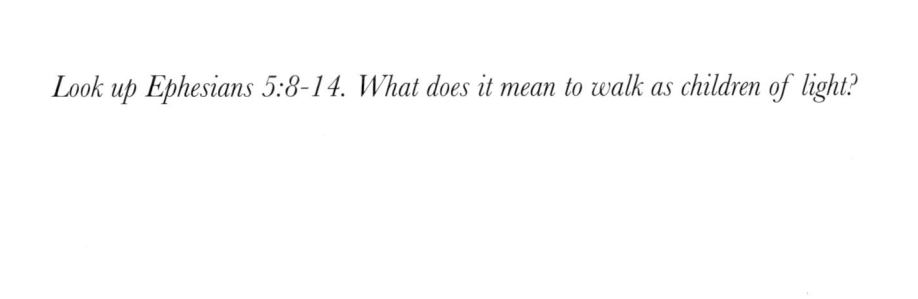

Look up Ephesians 5:8-14. What does it mean to walk as children of light?

What are the things that tempt you to not let your light shine?

How can you let your light shine this week?

YES
and
AMEN

WEEK THREE // DAY TWO

MATTHEW 5:17-20

The tone of the sermon begins to shift. Jesus had spent a lot of time telling the disciples about the character of a believer, and then He told them about the influence of the believer on the world around them. Now Jesus speaks of His own relationship with the law. Jesus says that He has not come to abolish the law and the prophets, but to fulfill them (Romans 8:3-4). But what does that mean? Jesus had spoken much of kingdom life, and yet He had not mentioned the law. He was showing that there was a shift happening. Disciples would hunger and thirst for righteousness, but not just through the law. Disciples would be changed from the inside out. That is what the Beatitudes were all about. Perhaps the crowds nearby were beginning to think that Jesus was advocating for the law to be thrown out with all His talk of inward transformation, but Jesus would tell them that is not what He was coming to do. Now Jesus makes the bold statement that He Himself was the fulfillment of the law.

The law and the prophets are speaking of the Old Testament Scriptures. Jesus makes it clear that these are not being done away with. In fact, for the believer, the Old Testament has an even greater significance as we see that every verse points to Jesus. He is the fulfillment of every prophecy, every type, and every word. He is the Passover Lamb. He is the mercy seat and the Holy of Holies. He is the tabernacle come to dwell among men. He is Immanuel. He is the promised One. He is the Sacrifice. He is the promised Deliverer. He is the fulfillment of every promise, every sacrifice, and every feast. From the first verses of Matthew, we are overwhelmed with how Jesus fulfills what the prophets had spoken (Matthew 1:22, 2:6, 15, 17, 23, 4:14). And Jesus Himself would declare that Moses wrote about Him (John 5:46). 2 Corinthians 1:20 will tell us that every promise of God finds its yes and amen in Jesus. He lived the perfect life that we could not live, and He died the death that we deserved. *He fulfilled every word of Scripture.*

Jesus goes on to declare again the ultimate power and authority of Scripture. Jesus' life does far from negate the need for the Old Testament. Jesus confirms our need for these holy words where every single part points to Jesus who is the fulfillment of it all. Many believers think that the Old Testament is irrelevant for the Christian, or that it is not as interesting as the New Testament. This is just *not* true. The Old Testament gives the New Testament such a depth of meaning. It is no wonder that the Greek word here for "fulfill" means "to make full, complete, or consummate." Jesus does all of these things. The Old and New Testaments must be viewed as gloriously whole, all pointing to the cross.

Jesus makes the bold statement that in order to enter the kingdom of heaven, a person's righteousness must exceed the righteousness of the scribes and Pharisees. We often have a negative view of the scribes and Pharisees, but we must remind ourselves that in the first century these were the most righteous people around. They were professionals at keeping the law. They followed every command and then added their own rules for good measure. These were the most religious men around. So when Jesus says that we must be more righteous than them, what is He saying? It certainly seems like an impossible task. Jesus was pointing out that in our own strength there is no way that we can ever measure up. Even the scribes and Pharisees only had an outward or external righteousness. They appeared to do all the right things, but their hearts were not following after God. Jesus is reminding them that He desires purity of heart and not just purity of actions. He is concerned not just with what we do, but with our motives as well. But there is good news. This righteousness can be achieved, not on our own, but because Christ has given us *His* righteousness. We receive this righteousness through Him. It has been imputed to us by Jesus (2 Corinthians 5:21). Jesus has fulfilled the law and has brought to us the new covenant that is now written on our hearts (Jeremiah 31:33). So we can now hunger and thirst for righteousness, because our hearts have been transformed (Matthew 5:6). We can be zealous for good works (Titus 2:14). Jesus has come to be our righteousness and to cause righteousness to grow inside of us because *He* is in us.

Look up Matthew 1:22, 2:6, 15, 17, 23, 4:14 and record some of the things that Jesus fulfilled.

Why is the Old Testament important for Christians?

What is the difference between the righteousness of the scribes and Pharisees and the righteousness of believers?

A HEART *of* ANGER

WEEK THREE // DAY THREE

MATTHEW 5:21-26

Jesus continues to go to the heart of the matter instead of just dealing with the surface issues. Jesus has now made the bold statement that in order to enter the kingdom of heaven, a person's righteousness must be greater than the scribes and Pharisees. Jesus was defying the culture of the day that believed that these men were the ultimate authority on life and Scripture. Immediately, Jesus brings their teaching into question. Over the coming verses, Jesus will show some contrasts of what the people had heard said, and then He will use the phrase, "but I say to you." Jesus is not contradicting the Old Testament Scripture, but He is instead bringing into question the perversion of it that had been perpetuated by the scribes and Pharisees. Jesus was speaking to people who did not read God's Word for themselves. During the time of the Babylonian captivity, the people had stopped speaking Hebrew which is what the Scriptures were written in, and instead they spoke the common languages. Because the people did not know Hebrew, they could not read or listen to the words of God in the Old Testament and they were dependent on the scribes and Pharisees to read and interpret it for them. Unfortunately, the scribes and Pharisees were much more concerned with outward appearances than inward holiness, and they often twisted the Scriptures and held only to the letter of the law without showing the depth of the spirit of the law. What a reminder to us of the importance of being in God's Word for ourselves and not just relying on what others have said about the Bible.

In the following verses, we see Jesus going deeper into what it means to be pure in heart. So Jesus calls into question the teaching on one of the most recognizable parts of the Ten Commandments when He brings up the commandment not to murder. Most people would hear that commandment and be tempted to check it off a list of commandments that they had kept perfectly. But Jesus had come to fulfill, to fill up, or deepen the law. Jesus would reveal that from the time those words had been uttered on another very important mountain, God had been seeking after the hearts of men, not just outward conformity to a set of rules. The command to not murder is in one very real way about not committing homicide, and yet its meaning goes far deeper than just that. It is a command to see other people as made in the image of God—a command for us to see value in all people, because God sees value in all people. You see, murder is not just something that happens with a weapon, it is any thought or action that seeks to destroy or tear down other people who have been made in God's image.

Both anger and murder reveal hearts that are not pure. And Jesus is the only one that can make our hearts pure before Him. Jesus is showing His disciples and the crowds looking on that anger impedes worship, and that our relationship with others impacts our relationship with God. We must be quick to deal with sin in our hearts and discord with other people. This is the purpose of the illustrations that Jesus gives. We must not let sin fester, or unforgiveness grow, or bitterness overtake us. God desires for hearts that are surrendered to Him and transformed from the inside out. We must allow God to transform not only our words and our actions, but our hearts.

The Sermon on the Mount, like all of Scripture, is not just a list of rules; it is full of principles to guide our hearts. We follow God, not just a set of rules. We must not, like the Pharisees, try to skate by with the bare minimum requirements, but instead come to the Lord with hearts that want to follow after Him. We must be willing to lay down our pride and ourselves and plead with Him to change us from the inside out.

These words only point us to Jesus and the message of the gospel. We cannot do this on our own. Yet Jesus paid the price we could not pay to reconcile us to God and man. He has poured out full, complete, unwavering forgiveness for every ounce of anger that stirs in our sinful hearts. We now have His imputed righteousness. And now He works in us to change and transform us from the inside out to be the people that He has called us to be.

*Why do we as humans prefer a set of outward rules instead of
the hard standards of inward holiness that God desires?*

*What are some ways that we murder the character
of other people with our thoughts and words?*

*What does God want our heart to be toward other people?
How can you put this into practice this week?*

THE HEART *of the* PROBLEM

WEEK THREE // DAY FOUR

MATTHEW 5:27-30

Jesus continues to deepen the meaning of the law and stand in contrast to the teachings of the Pharisees that sought to do just enough to get by without having a transformed heart. This time, Jesus will speak into the topic of lust and sin that is rooted in our hearts. Jesus does not merely talk about the sin that is seen outwardly, but He goes much deeper to the things that happen in our hearts. He is calling His people to be pure in heart, not just pure in action.

The Pharisees had taught that there was punishment for adultery, and that was true. But they saw no harm in lust and other impurity which were the things that led up to adultery. Jesus didn't want disciples that were simply robots that got as close as possible to the boundary lines of sin without stepping over. He desires His people to stay far from sin, and in this passage He speaks about the seriousness of sin. Jesus says that a person that looks at another with lustful intent has already committed adultery in their heart. He takes things so much deeper than what the Pharisees had been teaching. Jesus demanded purity of heart, not just purity of the body.

Perhaps lust and sexual sin are areas that you have to fight against, or perhaps there is another sin that seems to tempt you at every turn. The principle here regarding lust and sexual sin is so important, but we must also realize that Jesus isn't only talking about sexual sin. Jesus is talking about sin that makes us desires something that isn't ours—sin that makes us question if what God has given us is the best thing for us. This can manifest itself in many ways. We can lust after financial security, possessions, or someone's life situation. We can lust after someone's home, wardrobe, or social media following. We can even lust after wishing that our spouse was more romantic, or better at _____ (fill in the blank). The lusts of our heart are anything that makes us question if what we have is enough. This sin is *serious*. Sin is an accusation against God and His goodness. It is the belief that we know better than God does. And this sin of unbelief is a lack of trust in God whose plans and ways are so much higher than anything we can imagine.

Sometimes we look at the boundaries that have been set before us, and we worry that they are restricting us from something. But the boundaries that God has set in place give us freedom. God gives us boundaries because He knows what is best for us. We can flourish inside the boundary lines. A parent does not place a gate at the stairs to steal fun from their child, but to protect them and allow them to have freedom, joy, and safety. God does not restrict us from anything that is good for us. We must choose to trust that His boundaries are for our good.

Wrong thoughts lead to wrong actions. So we must guard our hearts and minds and fill them with the truth. We must allow our minds to be transformed so that we can become like Jesus and stand firm against the sin that tempts us to believe that we know better than God (Romans 12:1-2). God wants our hearts. He doesn't want us to just do the right things so we don't get in trouble. He wants us to chase after holiness because we love Him. The call of the believer is not simply to abstain from sin, but to pursue holiness, to pursue Christ-likeness. Sin is serious, and Jesus is serious about sin. The command in this passage to cast off parts of your body gives us a gruesome picture of the seriousness of our sinful condition. Jesus is not literally telling us to harm ourselves, instead He is telling us to do whatever it takes to rid your life of the sin that trips you up. In Colossians 3:5, Paul tells us to "put to death" the sin that is in us. We are called to a life of mortification—a life where we are constantly seeking to kill what is sinful and fleshly inside of us so that God can make us more like Himself. Jesus uses strong language to convince us to not mess around with sin.

Jesus is calling us to be pure in heart, because that is where blessing lies (Matthew 5:8). He is calling us to hate the sin that He has already died for. May we not continue in the sin that our Savior has suffered and died that we might be free from. The gospel compels us to look to the cross and be reminded of what sin cost. It compels us to run from sin. The gospel compels us not just to purity of action, but purity of heart.

How are our hearts and minds the root of our sin problems?

What things do you desire that are not yours?

How can you take action to put your own sin to death?
Pray now that God would help you to do that.

A Higher STANDARD

WEEK THREE // DAY FIVE

MATTHEW 5:31-37

The Pharisees were famous for searching for loopholes. They took God's good plan and searched for ways to get around what God had commanded. We see that in these verses as Jesus addresses marriage and divorce as well as oaths and keeping our word.

The culture of this time had a low view of marriage. Certain schools of thought in Judaism had made it so that a man could divorce his wife for just about any reason. If a husband didn't like his wife's cooking, he could divorce her. The culture had a low view of women and a low view of marriage, but Jesus had the opposite. I cannot speak to the issue of divorce without first recognizing that this is a difficult and often painful topic. Many, if not all, of us have been impacted by divorce in some way. As we read the words of Scripture, we must remember that God gives us guidelines for our good. He desires for us to flourish, and He seeks to set out the path by which we can flourish.

These words of Jesus regarding marriage remind us of the earlier words that Jesus spoke in the Beatitudes when He said, "Blessed are the merciful, for they shall receive mercy." A mark of Christian marriage is that it should be a place where grace and mercy are given freely, because we recognize that grace and mercy have been given freely to us. Some people have called this passage the exception clause. They label it as a place where Jesus outlines the acceptable reason for divorce, and yet if that is the only way that we view this passage, we are doing the same things that the Pharisees did and looking for the loopholes. Instead, as we look at this passage we must see that though the Pharisees were focused on divorce, Jesus was focused on marriage. Jesus was more focused on keeping marriages together than He was on all the possible reasons a spouse might be seeking to divorce.

Above all, marriage is designed to be a picture of Christ's relationship with His church. This is clearly illustrated for us in Ephesians 5:25-33. *Marriage should point us to the gospel.* When we think of our relationship with Christ, we are reminded of how many times we have failed Him, and yet still He has loved us and pursued us and kept covenant with us. 2 Timothy 2:13 tells us that if we are faithless, He is still faithful. What a picture for us to dwell on as we seek to live out marriages that point to the gospel. Though we fail our God often, He is abounding in steadfast love. He overflows with covenant-keeping, faithful forever, not going anywhere kind of love. There is much debate over the biblical grounds for divorce, and if remarriage is ever permissible.

Some believe that this passage permits divorce only in the case of adultery; other scholars point out that the wording used here is not the Greek for adultery, but for fornication which refers to sexual immorality before marriage, and is referring to the Jewish betrothal period. Whichever side you land on, this truth is clear, God never intends for marriage to end in divorce. John Piper in his wonderful book, *This Momentary Marriage*, said this, "The meaning of marriage is the display of a covenant-keeping love between Christ and his people... Marriage is patterned after Christ's covenant relationship to His redeemed people, the church. And, therefore, the highest meaning and the most ultimate purpose of marriage is to put the covenant relationship of Christ and his church on display. That is why marriage exists…The most important implication of this conclusion is that keeping covenant with our spouse is as important as telling the truth about God's covenant with us in Jesus Christ…It's about portraying something true about Jesus Christ and the way that He relates to His people. It is about showing in real life the glory of the gospel." May we be people that have a high and holy view of marriage just as Jesus does.

Jesus then speaks about oaths. And He simply instructs the disciples to be people of their word. He commands them to do what they say that they will do. Instead of looking for loopholes to not have to follow through, do what you have promised. In many ways, Jesus teaching on divorce and on oaths go together seamlessly. Jesus wants us to be people who keep our promises and by doing so, display how He keeps His promises to us.

Why do we as people often focus on the loopholes, instead of focusing on the commands? Do you think that our view would change if we could grasp that God desires for our good?

Read Ephesians 5:25-33. What is marriage to be a picture of?

How can marriage put the gospel on display?

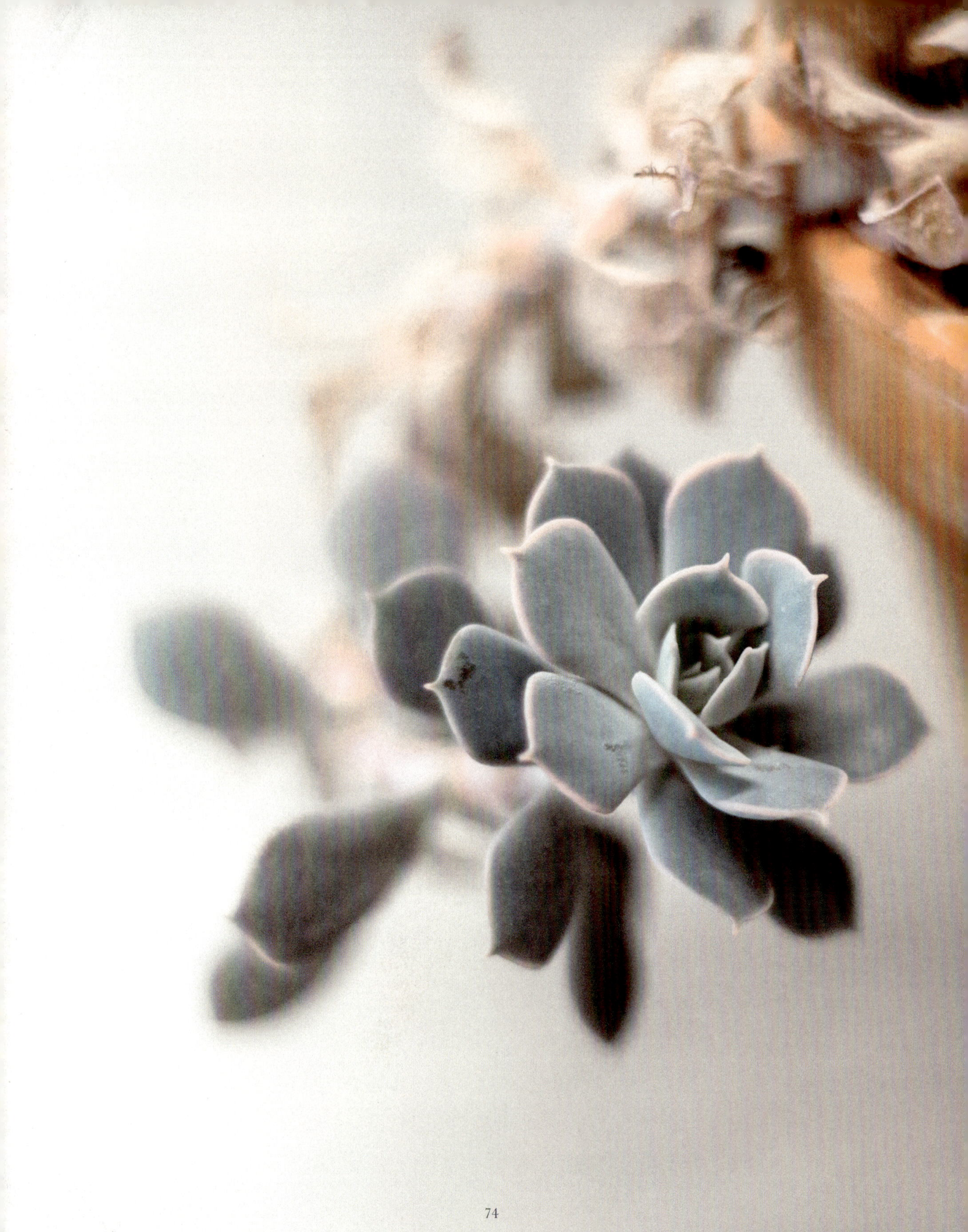

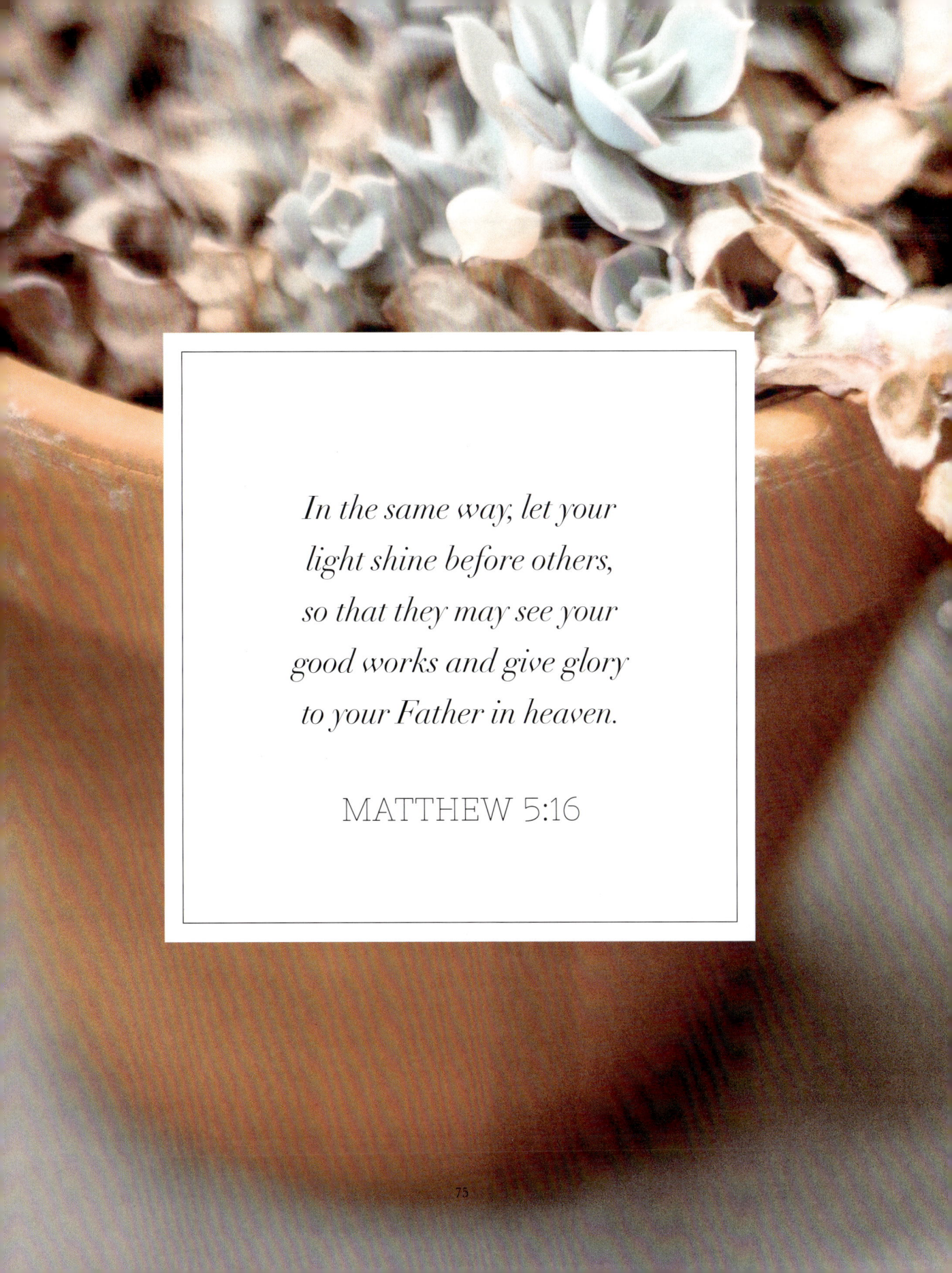

In the same way, let your light shine before others, so that they may see your good works and give glory to your Father in heaven.

MATTHEW 5:16

WEEKLY REFLECTION

WEEK THREE

Read Matthew 5:14-37

▶▶ *Paraphrase the passage from this week.*

▶▶ *What did you observe from this week's text about God and His character?*

▶▶ *What does the passage teach about the condition of mankind and about yourself?*

▶▶ *How does this passage point to the gospel?*

▶▶ *How should you respond to this passage? What is the personal application?*

▶▶ *What specific action steps can you take this week to apply the passage?*

The Gospel-Centered
LIFE

WEEK FOUR // DAY ONE

MATTHEW 5:38-48

The close of Matthew 5 contains some of the most perspective-shifting words of Jesus. Jesus is calling His people to a higher standard of living than comes naturally to us. We are familiar with many of the phrases that come from this section of the Sermon on the Mount. Phrases like, "an eye for an eye," "turn the other cheek" and, "go the extra mile" com to our minds. Yet living out the profound theological truths that these catchy phrases represent is so much more powerful than just saying a catchy phrase.

Jesus is teaching the disciples, and us, how to live the kingdom life. Jesus begins by referencing the Pharisees' interpretation of the law. "An eye for an eye" is a phrase used in the Old Testament in multiple passages (Exodus 21:24, Leviticus 24:20, Deuteronomy 19:21), and yet the Pharisees were again twisting the meaning of the passage. In the Old Testament, this was a protection against the exploitation of the weak and vulnerable. It was a way to make sure that the punishment fit the crime. In fact, this direction was given to judges, not individuals. The Pharisees had taken it as a way to exact revenge, when it was actually meant to protect the most vulnerable from harsh judgment. Our flesh likes to make things about revenge as well. We like things to be fair, but Jesus calls us to live so much higher than that. He calls us to be Christ-like. He calls us to be humble and sacrificial. We are not being told to be doormats, and we are certainly not being called to ignore violence, but instead He is calling us to be people of humility. He is calling us to be people that don't just demand their rights, but people who give up their rights for the good of others.

The Jews would have also been very familiar with the concept of going the extra mile. In the first century while they lived under Roman rule, Romans were allowed to demand that a Jew assist him for up to a mile. For the Jews, it was humiliating. It reminded them that they were not free men but were under the oppression of Rome. So when Jesus says to go two miles, He is instructing them to die to self and their own pride, and give freely. He then instructs them to give to the needy and the beggar. Jesus calls His people to live a life of grace and not judgment. Christians should show mercy and grace, because that is what has been shown to us.

Again, Jesus addresses the false interpretations of the Pharisees. Though the law did command Jews to love their neighbor, there was never a command to hate your enemy. Jesus again is calling the disciples to be Christ-like by telling them to love their enemies and pray for those that persecute them. It is hard to hate someone that you are actively praying for. Bonhoeffer said, "This is the supreme command. Through the medium of prayer we go to our enemy, stand by his side, and plead for him to God." This is the standard that we are being called to live by. Not a checklist or a moral playbook, but a heart that has been transformed by the beauty of the gospel and the grace that has been extended to us. Jesus tells us that Christians should be different than the rest of the world. We should be like Him.

We can only do these things when we die to self and pursue Jesus. We cannot do this in our own strength. It must be from an overflow of abiding in Him (John 15), and allowing Him to transform us. We should have the mark of our Father in heaven, a family resemblance when it comes to our Lord. As He transforms us into His image, we will stop living simply to please ourselves, but instead live lives that seek to serve those around us and glorify our Savior. When we stop being self-centered and start being Christ-centered, we will live a life that is gospel-centered.

How do people twist these popular phrases found here in the Sermon on the Mount?

How are these verses a command for us to be Christ-like?

Why can we not live like this in our own strength?
How does Christ-likeness come as a result of abiding in Jesus?

For His
GLORY

WEEK FOUR // DAY TWO

MATTHEW 6:1-4

As disciples of Jesus who have chosen to follow God, we come to this question—who will we live for? Will we follow God to bring glory to ourselves, or will we follow Him to bring glory to God alone? The Sermon on the Mount is teaching us that our why is just as important as our what. The reason we do things is as important and even more important than just the things that we do. We must guard our hearts and our motives for even the good things that we do. Our fallen nature means that even when we are doing good, we are usually filled with false motivations. Sometimes we are looking for the approval of others, sometimes for status, and other times for recognition. But the entire Sermon on the Mount is about calling us to a higher standard. So here we see Jesus calling the disciples to live for God's glory and not their own.

In chapter 6, Jesus will address several spiritual disciplines. He will speak of giving, praying, and fasting. In our modern culture, we often cringe at the word "discipline." It feels rigid to us to live a disciplined life. Yet we must note that as Jesus speaks of these areas of discipline, He never uses the word "if," but instead uses the word "when." Jesus expects us to live a life of discipline and service. The first area that He speaks of is giving to the needy.

Jesus says that when we give to the needy, we shouldn't make a big show of it. We shouldn't sound the trumpets and point all the attention to ourselves. Jesus says that this is what the hypocrites do. The word "hypocrite" was used at this time to speak of actors. The hypocrites were those that performed on the stage and those that wore masks. Our modern understanding of a hypocrite is derived from these early hypocrites. A hypocrite is someone who performs their life as if they are living on a stage. They live for others to see them. They wear a mask. They look one way on the outside, but underneath that mask is something completely different. Jesus is giving us a strong and powerful illustration. He is telling us to not live to put on a show before men. He is telling us to not act like one thing when our hearts are in a totally different place. He is telling us to not pretend that we are doing something for the good of others, or to serve the Lord, when we are actually doing it for popularity, acceptance, and recognition. *Ouch.* It is easy for us to spot hypocrisy in others, but we must examine our own hearts to see where a root of hypocrisy lives and confess it. Jesus is telling us to take a long, hard look at our own hearts and the reasons that we do what we do. In chapter 5, we learned that anger in the heart is the same root sin as murder and that lust makes us guilty of adultery of the heart. Again, we are being pointed back to a reminder to be pure in heart. Now we are seeing how that plays out in giving.

Not only does Jesus command them to not give to impress others, He also tells them not to give to impress themselves. Self-righteousness puts our eyes on ourselves instead of putting our eyes on Jesus. We have no righteousness in and of ourselves. And yet, the beauty of the gospel is that Jesus has clothed us in His righteousness. There is really no such thing as self-righteousness. The only righteousness is the righteousness of Christ. But sometimes we allow the pride in our hearts to build, and we begin to think that we can do good on our own. We begin to think that we are somehow better than other people. And the gospel is going to tell us that this is just not true. So we are going to have to preach the truth of the gospel to our hearts that are so prone to wander. We are going to have to remind ourselves that any good in us is only because of Him.

But the good news is—there is gospel-hope for the hypocrite. And that is good news because each one of us has struggled with this. We can run to Jesus again and again, and surrender to Him and allow Him to make our hearts pure. As we gaze at the the goodness of the gospel and the grace that has been lavished on us, our perspective will begin to shift as we realize that though we are weak and sinful, Jesus has loved us and called us to be His children, and now He is conforming us to His own image. We are going to have to stop living for the approval of men, so that we can live for the approval of God.

*Do you ever find yourself living for the approval of other people?
How can you shift your gaze back to the Lord in these areas?*

How can hypocrisy creep into your heart?

How does the gospel free our hearts from living to please others?

HUMBLE *and* BOLD

WEEK FOUR // DAY THREE

MATTHEW 6:5-8

How should we pray? As children of God, we have been given the great privilege of coming to God in prayer, and now Jesus will teach us to pray. Before Jesus teaches the disciples to pray by teaching them the Lord's prayer as a model prayer, He first tells them what *not* to do. These commands and instructions come after similar instructions on how we should give. And as is His pattern throughout the whole Sermon on the Mount, we see that these commands first and foremost deal with our hearts.

We are first commanded to not pray as the hypocrites. The Pharisees and hypocrites prayed to be seen by others. They prayed on the street corners to show that they were so spiritual, they could not even wait until they arrived at the synagogue. They want to be seen by other people as spiritual. Their focus is on their own glory, instead of on the glory of God. In contrast, the Gentiles were known for praying "empty phrases," or "vain repetitions." The emphasis here is not that their prayer was repetitive, but that it was vain. They said words with no thought or heart behind them. They did what they perceived they were supposed to do. They were reciting spiritual words, but their hearts were not communing with God.

Jesus is dealing here with a heart issue. He is addressing not just the sin of the hypocrite and the Gentile; He is speaking into our own predisposition to sin. Martyn Lloyd Jones said, "Sin is something that follows us even into the very presence of God." What a sobering thought that our sin is so deeply rooted in our hearts that even when we come in prayer, our nature is to sin in coming. Both the Pharisee and the Gentile had the same problem. They were both self-centered and self-focused. For the Pharisee, this came out as a desire to please and impress other people. For the Gentile, it came out as a desire to say and do the right thing. He focused on doing it right instead of on a heart surrendered to God. Jesus is reminding us that prayer is about God's glory and not our own. He is revealing the truth that often when we come in prayer, we are still focused on ourselves. He is reminding us that it is about surrendered hearts and not about saying the right things. Even when we pray in secret, we can fall into the same trap of wanting people to know that we have spent time in prayer, or wanting to be recognized for our spirituality. We must not take this so far as to never pray in public or encourage and exhort other believers. Instead, we must focus on what Jesus is focusing on—the posture of our hearts as we come in prayer.

At its core, prayer is a wrestling. It is about us wrestling with our own fleshly nature. It is about submitting to the Lord. It is about seeking His glory and not our own. It is about coming in confession and being honest with both God and ourselves. It is about laying down our own plan and will, so that we can submit our hearts to His perfect plan. How easy it is for us to make idols of ourselves. We focus so much on the way that we want things done, and we get frustrated when things don't go the way that we had planned. Prayer is meant to align our hearts to the Lord so that we can take our eyes off of ourselves and fix our gaze on Him.

Verse 8 tells us that our Father knows what we need before we even ask Him. We could be tempted to wonder what the point is in praying if He already knows. We do not pray to make sure that He knows what is going on in our lives—He already knows. We do not pray to try to convince Him of our perspective or manipulate Him to act in our favor. Prayer aligns our hearts to God and to His kingdom purposes.

So we should come in prayer with great humility and with great boldness. We come because He has asked us to come. We come because we don't know where else to turn. We come because we know that He will do abundantly more than we could ever ask or think (Ephesians 3:20). We come because we know that we will find shelter for our souls in the presence of our God.

What did you learn about how we should and shouldn't pray from these verses?

How should prayer align our hearts to God and His kingdom purpose?

How can you pray differently in light of Jesus' instruction on how to pray?

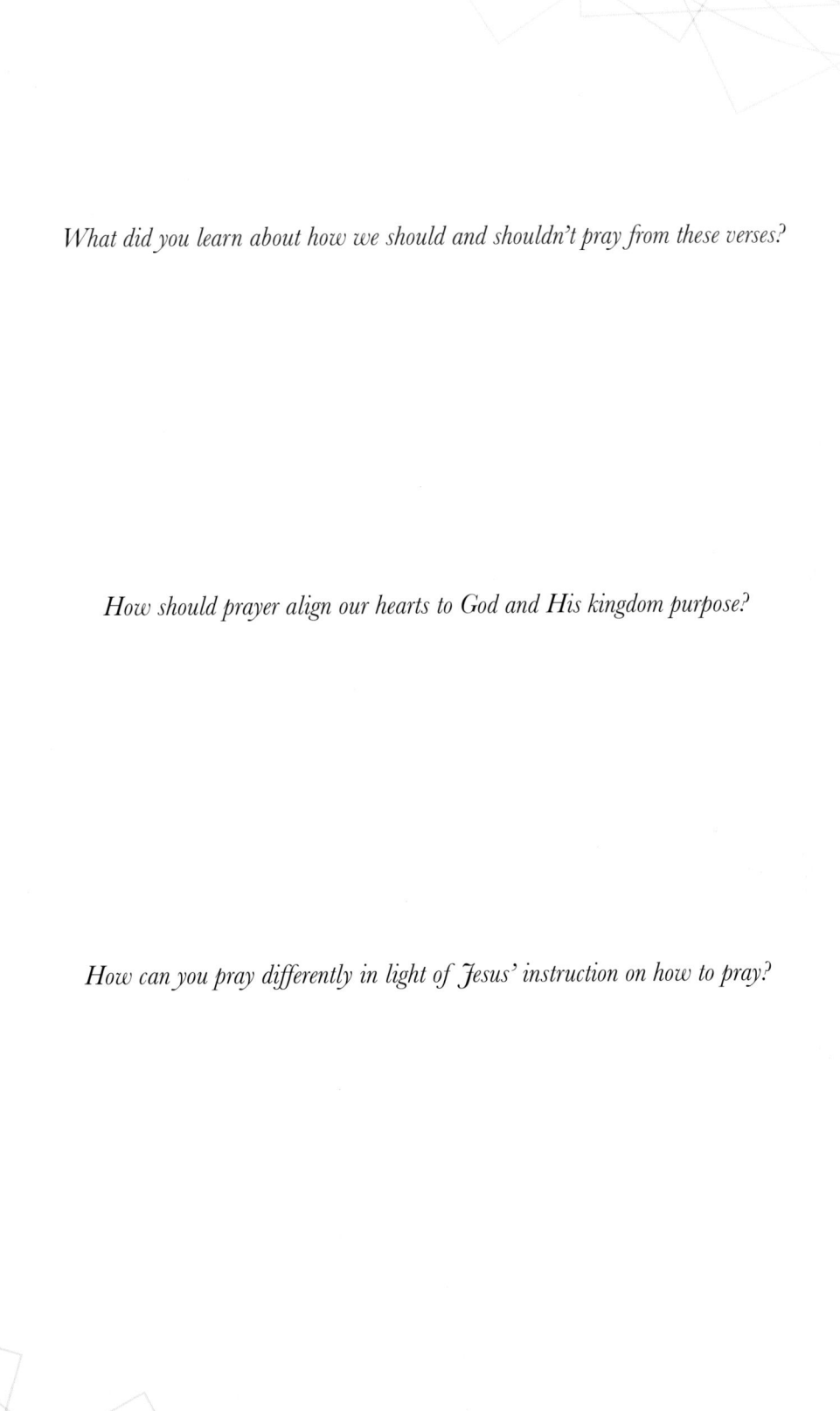

The Lord's
PRAYER

WEEK FOUR // DAY FOUR

MATTHEW 6:9-15

Our God already knows everything that we need, and yet He invites us to come to Him in prayer. He invites us to enter His presence and stand in awe of His glory. Martyn Lloyd-Jones said, "Man is at his greatest and highest when, upon his knees, he comes face-to-face with God." Prayer is coming to God and choosing to align our hearts to who He is and to His will instead of our own. So this model prayer taught by Jesus is one that encompasses everything that we ought to pray in just a few short lines. This prayer is an outline of the things that we should pray. That doesn't mean that we must simply recite these words, but that we can use this as instruction for the things that should be on our lips as we come to God in prayer.

He is Our Father. He is a God who is personal and who deals with His people. This is a reminder of both His individual love for us, as well as His love for the community of His people in the church. He is our loving and personal Father, and He is also the God who is in heaven. He is personal and He is majestic, and this is the great mystery that our high and holy God desires to meet with us in prayer. We ask to be reminded of His holiness. It is not that we are praying that His name could be anymore hallowed or holy, but instead that we are asking Him to help us see who He really is. We want to see His glory and His holiness. We come to Him asking for Him to align our hearts to seek His glory alone. Because when we recognize who He is, it will set all other areas of our lives into proper perspective.

We have already seen how integral the kingdom message is to the entire book of Matthew and to the Sermon on the Mount. It should come as no surprise then that this model prayer includes mention of the kingdom of God. We are to pray for His kingdom to come. The kingdom of God was inaugurated at the first coming of Christ, and now we wait for the consummation of that kingdom when He comes again. The Lord's prayer gives us a gospel focus. It focuses our hearts on the glory of God, and even our petitions are aligned with God's purpose and plan. In prayer, we set our hearts to His will and not our own. We actively seek His will by actively seeking Him through His Word. Each aspect of this prayer has practical implications for our lives right now. It isn't just about the future, but about our present. We do not simply seek after His future will, but we do today what He has called us to do. His will is not a mystical unknown thing. He has made it known to us in His Word, so our duty is to study His Word so that our hearts will be united to His. In this prayer, the first and foremost focus is on the glory of God. Prayer is not about requests, though He invites us to ask from Him. Prayer is about a heart that is steadfastly fixed on God's glory and His perfect plan. God's glory is our highest calling. The Westminster Shorter Catechism reminds us that "Man's chief end is to glorify God and to enjoy Him forever." So prayer should be focused on God because all things flow from Him.

The Lord's prayer has three petitions, and these requests sum up all that we ask from the Lord and also point us to the triune nature of our God. These requests cover every area of the life of a believer. John Stott put it this way, "What we are doing whenever we pray this prayer is to express our dependence upon God in every area of our human life. Moreover, a Trinitarian Christian is bound to see in these three petitions a veiled allusion to the Trinity, since it is through the Father's creation and providence that we receive our daily bread, through the Son's atoning death that we may be forgiven and through the Spirit's indwelling power that we are rescued from the evil one." This prayer points us to the gospel. It reminds us that God has created all things for His glory. It reminds us of our own weakness and need for forgiveness as it reminds us of the fall. It fills us with the comfort of redemption as we are reminded that in Christ's death on the cross we have received redemption and forgiveness. It helps us to live in light of the gospel as we interact with those around us by forgiving as we have been forgiven, and as we seek to know Him and live out His will. And it points us to the hope of the restoration to come when Jesus comes again and His kingdom comes forever and fully.

The Lord's prayer propels us to a gospel-centered view of God, it compels us to gospel-centered living, and it fills us with gospel-hope.

How does prayer align our hearts to God?

What phrase of the Lord's prayer stuck out most to you in your study?
Did you have any misconceptions about the Lord's prayer before studying it?

Paraphrase the Lord's prayer and then pray through the prayer.

For Him
ALONE

WEEK FOUR // DAY FIVE

MATTHEW 6:16-18

Again we are drawn back to the heart of the matter which is our own hearts. Jesus has touched on many topics in this sermon, and yet above all, He is calling us to have hearts that are pure before God and that are kingdom-focused. In this passage, Jesus speaks of how we should operate when we fast. We must again take note that Jesus assumes that we are fasting by using the word "when," instead of "if." Jesus did not have a problem with the fact that the hypocrites were fasting, but with the *way* that they were doing it. The problem with the fasting of the Pharisees was that they were doing it to be seen by other people. They were doing it to make themselves look good, instead of doing it to draw near to God. The purpose of fasting is to seek the Lord, to come in confession, to seek direction, and to pursue self-control. Yet the Pharisees made this act of worship a religious show. They were more concerned about their reputation than adoration.

The word "hypocrite" as we mentioned earlier was used of those that wore masks and performed on the stage. And the fasting of the hypocrites was also a performance. They were not humble and pure in heart before the Lord. They did what they thought they were supposed to do. They did it to impress others and to make themselves look good. They wanted to be noticed by others and thought of as holy, so they would make it very obvious when they were fasting. They would make themselves look hungry and sad, and would even spread ashes on their faces to show how difficult it was to fast. In contrast, Jesus tells us that when we fast, that we should go on like usual and not make a big deal about it. We don't need to announce our spirituality to be truly spiritual. Though there is great value in living as lights in this world, we must keep our hearts in check. Again this is a *heart* issue. We shine as lights in the world when we live righteously for God alone. We become a hypocrite when we try to practice so-called righteous deeds so that we will be seen by others and thought of as holy by men. When our spirituality is a performance, we are likely being hypocritical. When our public prayers and our private prayers are very different, we may be being hypocritical. When we catch our hearts longing for the praise and recognition of other people, we must check our hearts. Though it may play out in different ways in our modern culture, we must be cautious of the same heart attitude. We must be careful to not flaunt our spirituality to impress others or make ourselves look good. We must guard our hearts from an attitude that thinks that if we do what is right, God will owe us, or fall into a mindset that thinks that favor with God is based on our own performance. Instead, we must seek after the Lord with our whole hearts. We must surrender our reputation and our pride and seek for His glory alone. These words are a fitting reminder after the Lord's prayer because again they call us to align our hearts to the Lord and to pray for His kingdom and not our own.

Jesus is calling us a higher standard. He is calling us to live for an audience of *one*. He is calling us to live a life where we do not focus on what other people will think of us, where we don't focus on what we think of ourselves, but where we focus on following after the Lord with an undivided heart. This is what it means to be pure in heart. And there is reward in following Him with all of our hearts for His glory alone. The reward may not come in the form of prestige or a platform. It may not come as honor and social media followers. It may not even come in this life. It may not come the way that we expect, and that is what life in the upside-down kingdom is all about. Jesus is calling us higher—calling us to a life where we live for Him alone.

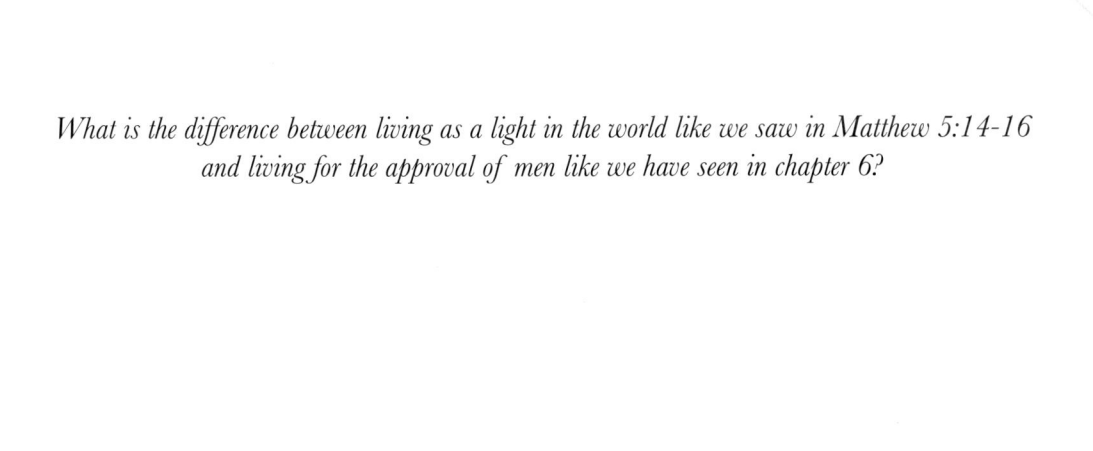

What is the difference between living as a light in the world like we saw in Matthew 5:14-16 and living for the approval of men like we have seen in chapter 6?

Where do you sometimes look to for approval?

How does this passage realign your heart to look to God alone for approval?

Our Father in heaven,
your name be honored as holy.
Your kingdom come.
Your will be done
on earth as it is in heaven.

MATTHEW 6:9b–11a

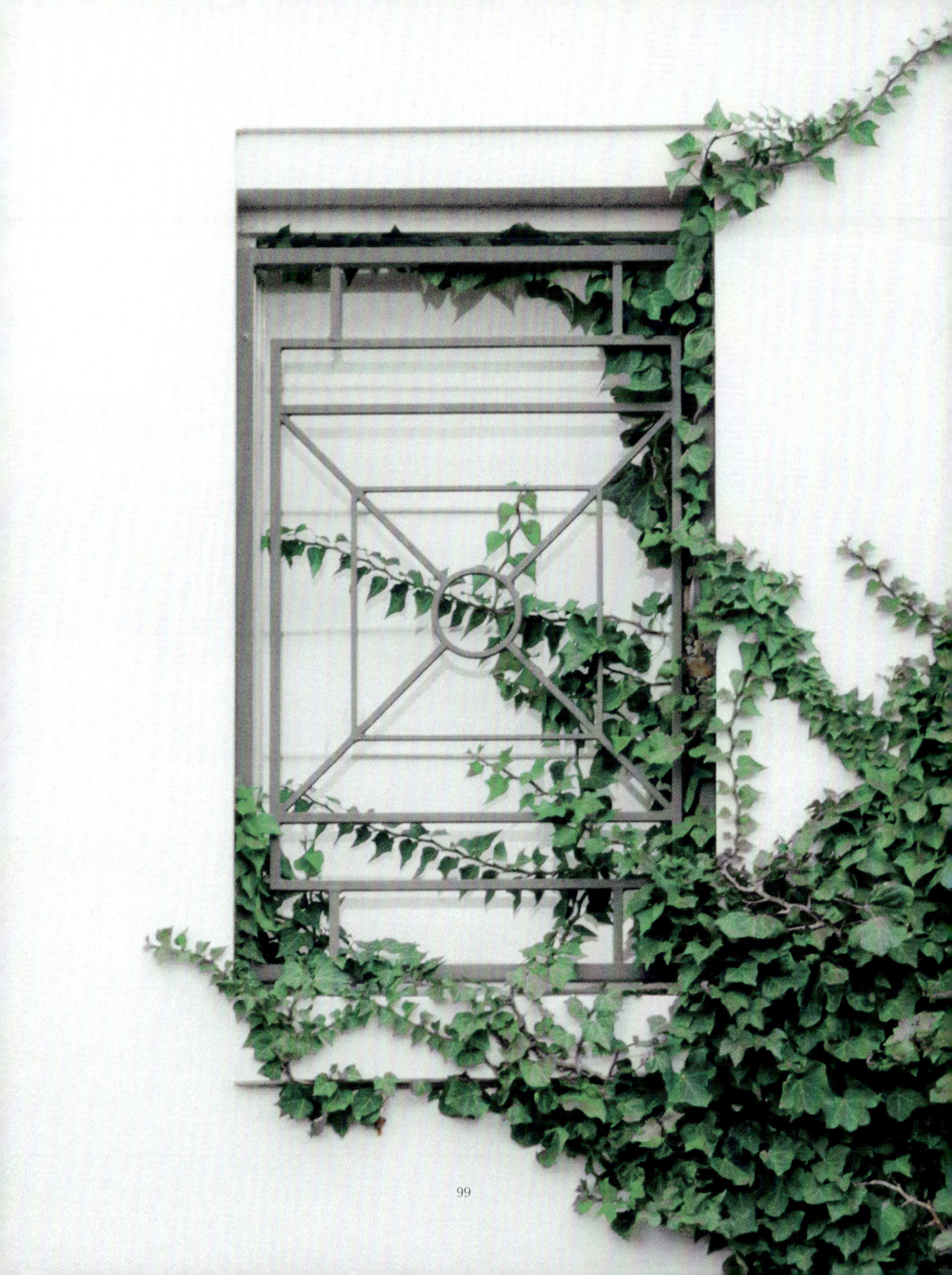

WEEKLY REFLECTION

WEEK FOUR

Read Matthew 5:38-6:18

▸▸ *Paraphrase the passage from this week.*

▸▸ *What did you observe from this week's text about God and His character?*

▸▸ *What does the passage teach about the condition of mankind and about yourself?*

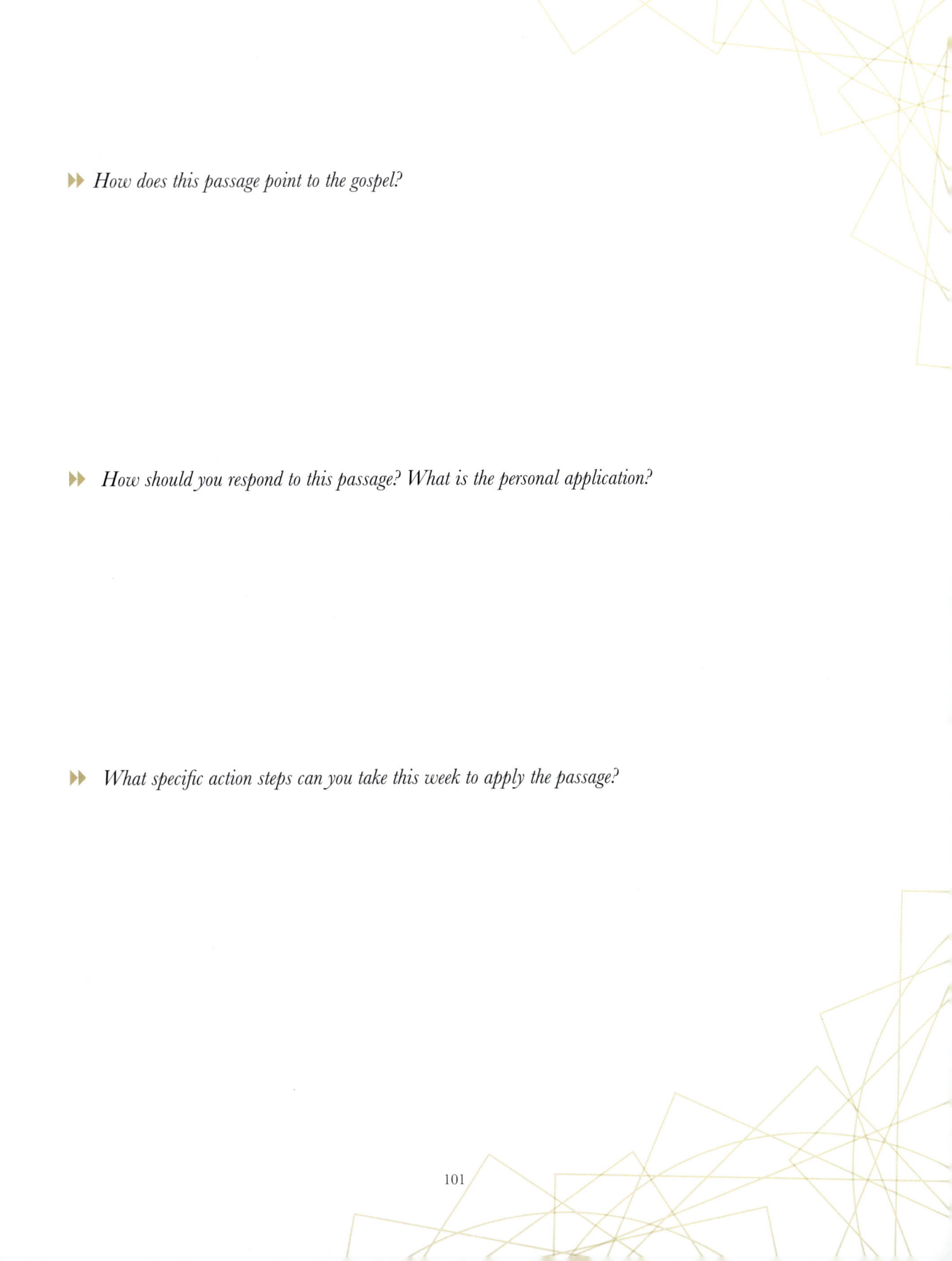

▶▶ *How does this passage point to the gospel?*

▶▶ *How should you respond to this passage? What is the personal application?*

▶▶ *What specific action steps can you take this week to apply the passage?*

TREASURES *of the* HEART

WEEK FIVE // DAY ONE

MATTHEW 6:19-24

What do you treasure? What are your greatest ambitions? Who is your master? These are the questions that Jesus is asking in this passage. The focus of the sermon is seamlessly shifting from hypocrisy to anxiety. And yet with both of these things the problem can be boiled down to an excessive focus on self. The hypocrite is concerned about his reputation and what other people think of him. The anxious person is concerned about just about everything. The anxious person thinks that everything depends on them, and they are crushed under the heavy weight of this burden that was never meant for them to bear. This is about a heart issue. It is the question of where our affection is found. Will we focus on the things of self and this world, or will we shift our gaze heavenward and focus on the things of eternal value?

We may be tempted to think that the cure for this anxiety is simply positive thinking. Sinclair Ferguson points out, "Jesus teaching, then, is not a form of 'the power of positive thinking.' The problem with anxious people is not merely that they think negatively about life. It is more radical than that. Anxious people think *untheologically* about life!" We don't need positive thinking—we need theological thinking. We don't need inspirational words—we need God's Word. We don't need to be told that we are enough—we need to be pointed to Jesus who is more than enough. Our theology is what we believe about God, and we need to allow the truth that we know about God and who He is to impact every area of our lives. We need to rest in His provision and His character instead of being sucked into a culture that is going to tell us that we can have "do it yourself" success. We must let our theology dictate every part of how we think, speak, and act.

Jesus points us to the truth that upside-down priorities cause anxiety. He urges us to put our hope in the things that last. He urges us to build *His* kingdom. He compels us to invest in His kingdom and not the kingdom of this world. We are compelled to pour our energy and invest our time into the things that are eternal. When Jesus speaks of not laying up your treasures on earth, but instead laying them up in heaven, He is not merely speaking of money. He is focusing us in on the things that pull for our attention and affections. The problem is not having money or things, but being consumed by them. Whether you have wealth, or you don't have it, don't let it's pursuit have a hold on you. Martyn Lloyd-Jones points out that "Our Lord is concerned here not so much about our possessions as with our attitude towards our possessions." We are being urged toward a heavenly focus and lives that steward whatever we have been entrusted with well. The enemy here is not just money or possessions, but anything that pulls for our affection. We must guard our hearts from anything that pulls our heart from the Lord. These are the things that become idols of our hearts, and so often they are centered on ourselves.

Spiritual vision and ambition changes our perspective on life. We must remember that there is no division between the sacred and the secular. For the child of God, everything is sacred, because everything can be done for God's glory. So the teaching here is not to sell all that we have and give away every dollar and not prepare for the future. The principle is for us to live with our eyes focused on the eternal. We must fix our gaze on Jesus and ask Him to turn our eyes away from worthless things and toward Him (Psalm 119:37). Whether we are studying Scripture, washing dishes, or working at our job, we can live for the eternal. Whether we have great wealth, or small amount of money, we can steward it in a way that honors God and places our focus on the things that matter most. We plead with God to turn our eyes from things that will fade away, and pour our hearts into pursuits that will yield eternal value.

What are the treasures of your heart? Write them down. Resist the urge to only list the good things. Write down the things that pull for your attention and sometimes seek to pull your affection from Christ.

When we think that everything depends on us, our hearts are filled with anxiety and worry. How does trusting the Lord alleviate that burden?

How does theological thinking change our perspective? What truths about God can change your perspective today on your life or current situation?

HIS EYE
is on the
SPARROW

WEEK FIVE // DAY TWO

MATTHEW 6:25-31

Do not be anxious. Those words seem to fall into the "easier said than done" category. Worry and anxiety plague our culture, and Christians are in no way exempt from the inclination to worry. Yet Jesus commands us so clearly *not* to be anxious. He tells us not to be anxious, but He doesn't just leave us there. He shows us the state we are in and diagnoses our condition, and then He quickly points us to the cure for the worry that plagues us. Our tendency is to worry about every little thing, but instead Jesus tells us to think on who He is. We need the truth of Scripture to combat worry and help us view life from God's perspective. Jesus tells us that in order for us to change our anxiety, we are going to need to change our thinking. The renewal of our mind and the process of sanctification begin with our thoughts (Romans 12:2), so we must allow Jesus to change our thinking.

Worry is a lack of trust. When we choose to worry, we are choosing not to trust that God is in control. In this sense it is a faulty view of God that allows our hearts to worry. If we could see and know who God is, we would not worry about a single thing because we would be utterly convinced of His sovereignty over everything. We think that things depend on us, but we can't even take a single breath without Him. That should cause us to have a big sigh of relief. He is in control of every breath, and He can certainly handle the problems of our life. Our view of God will impact whether or not our hearts are filled with worry, and the best way to ensure that we have a proper view of God is to immerse ourselves in Scripture. We can choose to view God as a fearful tyrant, or we can see from Scripture that He is actually a loving Father and take comfort in that truth. Our enemy wants us to view our God as the fearful tyrant. He wants us to doubt God's goodness and question His love for us. This has been his tactic from the beginning. In the garden, Satan tempted Eve by making her question what God had said. He made her question if God really loved her and if He was really out for her best interest. These same questions may pop into our hearts even if they are never uttered from our lips. We wonder, *Does God love me? Can He be trusted? Has He forgotten me? Does He have a good plan for my life? If He has a good plan for my life, why am I facing _____?* We are suspicious of God because of our sinful nature. But the opposite of this sneaky and sinful suspicion of God is faith. Jesus calls for us to look at the birds. God cares for them, and you are so much more important to the Father than birds. Instead of trying to control, seek the One who is in control. These verses point us right back to the Lord's prayer and this wrestling and struggling in prayer. We must come and lay down our worry and rest by faith in the plan that He has.

These verses are not teaching that we should not plan, work, or save for the future. The birds that are mentioned still work and gather their food. Planning is good, worrying is bad. There is nothing wrong with working and saving and preparing; but when it crosses into anxious obsession, we know that things have gotten out of control.

The problem is misplaced desires. This passage begins with the word "Therefore," and it builds on the verses before it. Jesus is calling us to take a look at the things that we seek. Do we seek after the material things of this world, or do we seek things above (Colossians 3:2) Do we seek after the good gifts, or do we seek the One who is the Giver of all things? We must surrender our lesser pursuits and seek after the One who has sought us. We must lay down our worry and anxiety at the feet of Jesus and trust Him. Martyn Lloyd-Jones said, "There is no circumstance or condition in this life which should lead a Christian to worry." What a true statement. Our God is in control of it all. He knows the end from the beginning. *He is sovereign over it all*. As the world shifts and changes, He remains ever the same, and we can trust Him.

The same Greek word, merimnao, that is translated as "anxious" in this passage appears again in the story of Mary and Martha. Read Luke 10:38-42. Martha was distracted, anxious, and troubled. How does the impulse to do it all leave us feeling the same way as Martha? How does trust in God transform us?

How does a right view of God put our worry into perspective?

Read Romans 8:31-39. How does this passage give us comfort in any situation?

SEEK

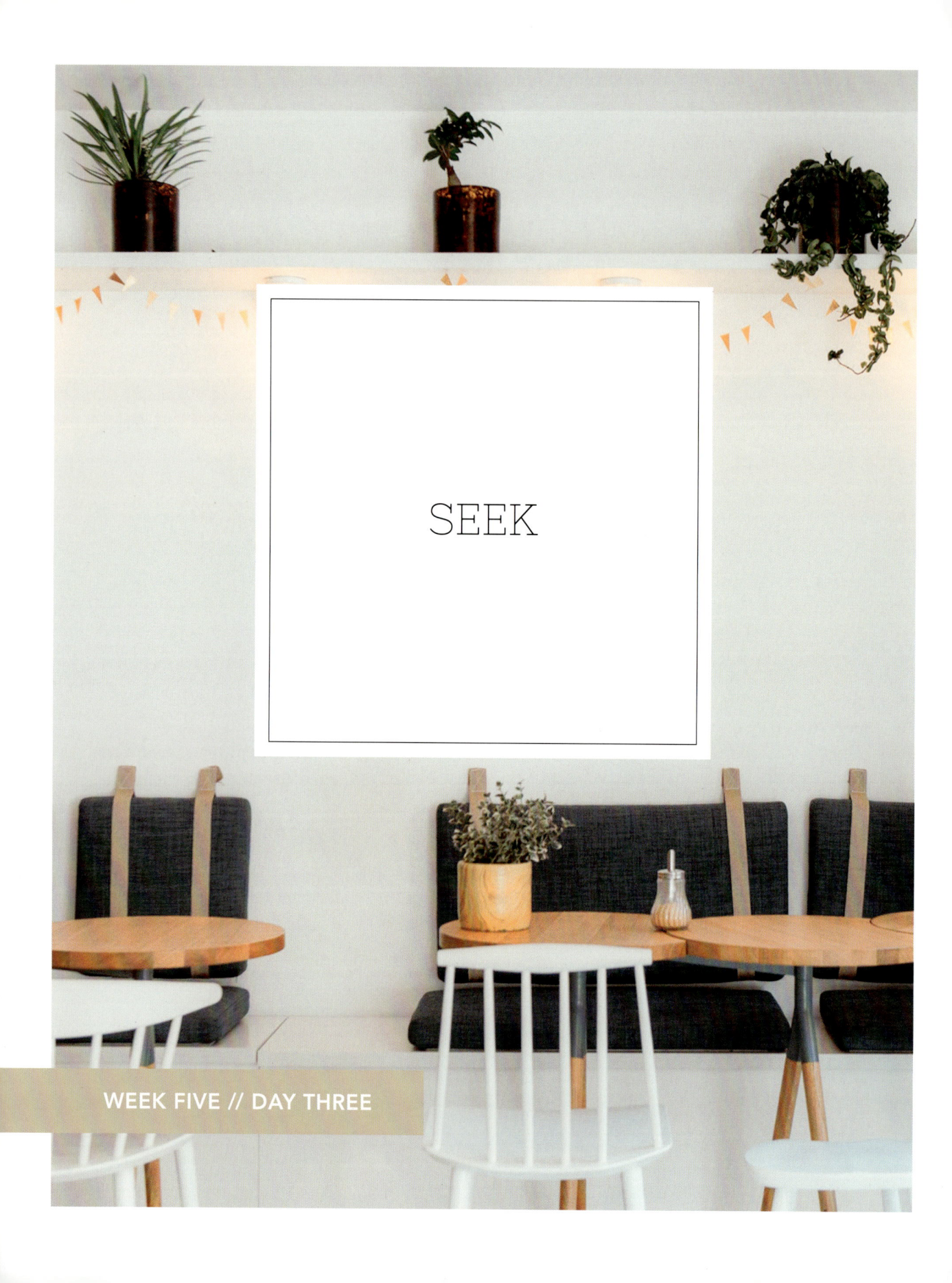

WEEK FIVE // DAY THREE

MATTHEW 6:32-34

What do you seek? What do you desire? We know the "right" answer to these questions, but we must examine our hearts to see if our life and actions line up with the truth that we know. We find in this passage a contrast. Jesus has just talked about worry and anxiety, and now He is contrasting what unbelievers seek after and what believers should seek after. Jesus is giving us clear instruction on what our focus should be, so we had better listen up.

Jesus tells us that our natural and human inclination is to seek after "all the things." We seek after all those things that cause us to worry. We seek after food and clothing. We seek after control and prestige. We seek to do it ourselves. And Jesus is telling us here that our natural inclination is all wrong. We worry about things that God has already got under control. We want things in our timing and in the way that we think is best. But Jesus tells us that our Father knows exactly what we need. We can trust Him to provide what is best for us, and we can trust Him to provide it at the perfect time. That may mean that we will face a season of waiting. It may mean that we will not understand. But it also means that He will be faithful.

Verse 33 shows us the contrast though. Jesus has told us what not to focus on, and now He tells us what we should be focused on. We can't add an inch to our height. We can't guarantee an easy life. We can't make other people think highly of us. But we can surrender to Him. We should seek first (or above all) His kingdom and His righteousness. Our greatest desire should be to see God's plan accomplished. We are being commanded to focus on what matters. To set our gaze on things that have eternal value. To trust that when we seek Him, He will take care of the details. Seeking first the kingdom means that there is nothing more that we want than God's will. We are willing to surrender our own plans so that His plan can go forth. This means that our heart beats for the gospel to go forth. John Stott said, "The kingdom spreads only as the gospel of Christ is preached, heard, believed, and obeyed." Being kingdom-focused is about fixing our eyes on Jesus and then seeking to do our part to spread the good news of the gospel.

Not only should we seek His kingdom, but also His righteousness. We should "hunger and thirst for righteousness" as we saw in Matthew 5. We should be consumed with knowing who He is so that we can become more like Him. And in seeking His kingdom and His righteousness, we will see that our worries will fade into the background as our focus is set on Him alone. Jesus is calling us to lay aside the things that do not matter, and focus on the things that matter for eternity. He is calling us to a purpose that is higher than anything we could think or imagine. He can take us ordinary people and use us for His extraordinary purposes when we will surrender to Him and focus our gaze on Him alone.

When we seek Him, we can let Him take care of the rest. We don't have to be anxious about tomorrow, because we have a God who is already there. He knows what is ahead, and He is already there preparing the way for us. God already knows everything that we need, and this frees us up to trust Him.

So seeking Him is really about surrender. We don't need to try harder or do better. We just need to surrender. We don't need to figure it all out, we just need to trust. We don't need to have a perfect plan, we need to trust the One who already does.

What does it mean to seek God in your daily life?

What are the things that prevent us from seeking and trusting Him?
What are the things that you are prone to worry about?

How does this passage point back to the upside-kingdom that Jesus has been teaching about?

JUDGE NOT

WEEK FIVE // DAY FOUR

MATTHEW 7:1-6

We have come to Matthew 7 which is the last chapter of the Sermon on the Mount. We have seen so much about who we should be and what life in God's kingdom should look like. We begin chapter 7 with some very familiar words. They are used often but not always used correctly. But since we have been studying this sermon for weeks now, we have the ability to look at these words in the direct context that Jesus spoke them which should help us understand what they mean. This section begins with Jesus saying, "Judge Not." These words have been quoted and twisted by both believers and unbelievers. Yet we will see that they fit perfectly in the context of this sermon and what Jesus has been teaching all along.

This message is quite similar to the beatitude that told us that "Blessed are the merciful, for they shall receive mercy." We learned there that the meaning was not that God would not be merciful to us if we were not merciful to others, but that the message was that if we are not merciful to others, we are showing that we have no understanding of the mercy that we have been shown. The meaning here is the same. Jesus is not telling us to not be discerning; in fact later in this section we will see Him very clearly tell us the importance of discernment. Instead, He is telling us that in light of all that we have been forgiven when we were worthy of judgement we should be gracious and merciful with others.

So often we tend to deal harshly with the sin of others and mercifully with our own sin. We make excuses for our personal sin, and we are harsh and critical at the slightest sin of others. Jesus is telling us that we have it all backwards. We should be diligent to rid our personal lives of sin, and we should be gracious with those around us. So often we mask our own guilt by deflecting our attention and even the attention of others to the sin of other people. Jesus would rather us take a long, hard look at our own sin, than at the sin of other people. When we do this, we are showing a lack of understanding as to the depths of the forgiveness that has been lavished on us. The sin of others should not lead us to feeling self-righteous, but remind us of our depravity and the great mercy and grace that we have been given.

The famous illustration to remove the log in our own eye before the speck in our brother's is a reminder that we must examine our own hearts. When we examine our hearts, we will find that we fall woefully short, and it is then that we can be reminded of the amazing grace of Jesus that has forgiven us and is in the process of making us more like Him. Jesus uses this vivid picture and then calls those that do this hypocrites. The word "hypocrite" is not foreign to the sermon. Jesus is telling us over and over again that the focus is not just outward conformity, but inward holiness. Jesus doesn't just want us to change what we do, He wants to change who we are.

So Jesus is calling us to lay down our critical and harsh spirits. He is asking us to view people the way that He views people. He is asking us to grow in sanctification and be more like Him. And the good news is that He never leaves us to do that on our own. He walks with us every step of the way to make us more like Him.

The last verse of this section may throw us off a bit. What is Jesus referring to when he references dogs and pigs? Jesus is referring to those who hear and repeatedly reject the precious message of the gospel. As believers, we are to take the gospel to every person (Matthew 28:19-20), but Jesus is telling them to not get discouraged when some people reject the precious message that they bring. Instead they can shake it off and move on to those that will accept this precious gift. Again, Jesus is after the heart. He tells them to go and tell everyone, and then when some reject the message, don't get discouraged by that. Get back up and go and tell someone else. Jesus is teaching us about life in His kingdom. He doesn't sugar-coat it or tell us there will never be hardship, or that we will never struggle with our own sin, but He reminds us that He is our true hope.

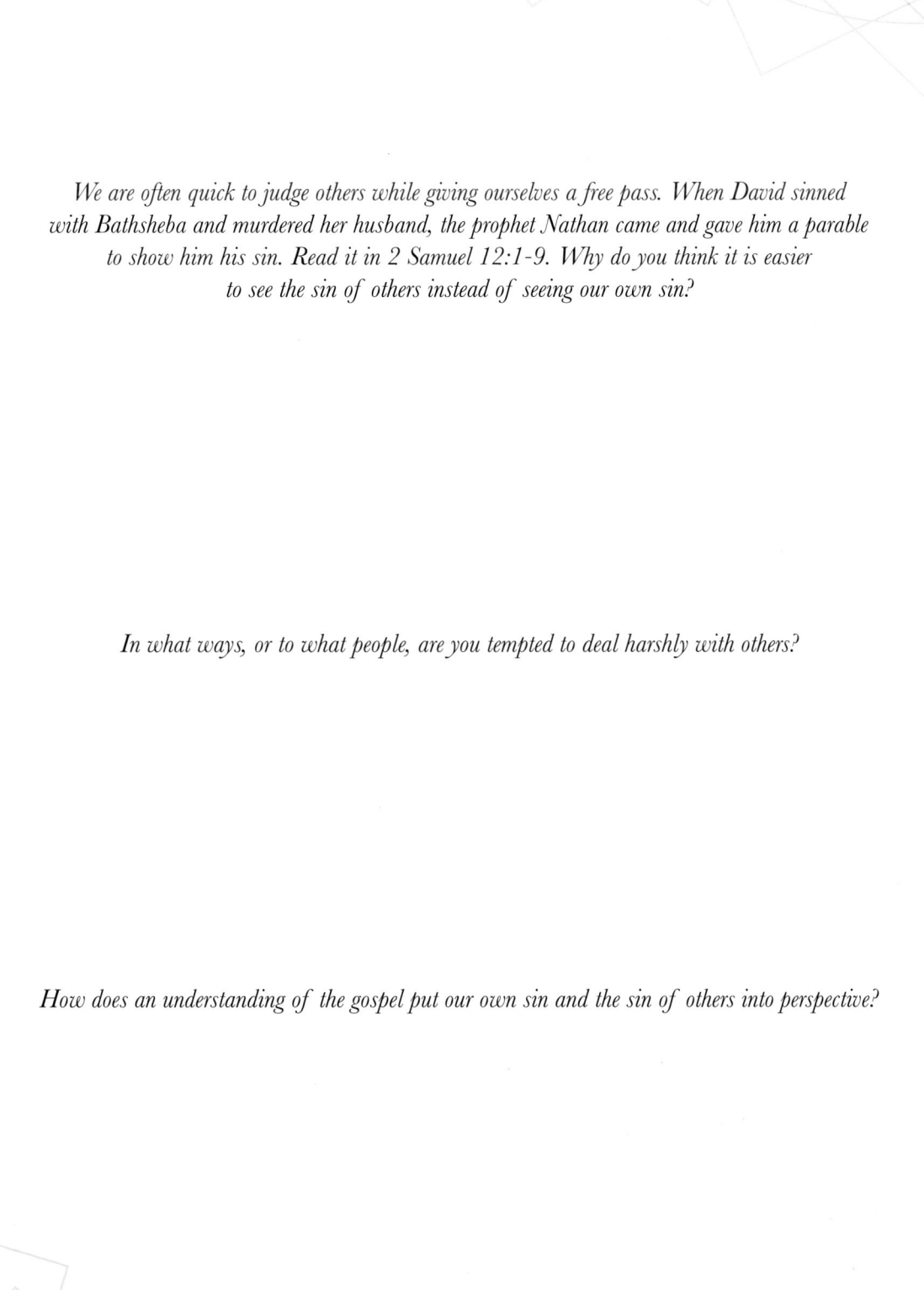

We are often quick to judge others while giving ourselves a free pass. When David sinned with Bathsheba and murdered her husband, the prophet Nathan came and gave him a parable to show him his sin. Read it in 2 Samuel 12:1-9. Why do you think it is easier to see the sin of others instead of seeing our own sin?

In what ways, or to what people, are you tempted to deal harshly with others?

How does an understanding of the gospel put our own sin and the sin of others into perspective?

ASK, SEEK, KNOCK

WEEK FIVE // DAY FIVE

MATTHEW 7:7-12

I have heard it said that the only things promised in this life are death and taxes, and though it certainly may seem that way sometimes, I think there are a lot of things we can add to that list as believers. At the top of the list of things that I am assured of is the faithfulness of God. He will keep His promises and do what He has said, and I think these verses are the perfect reminder of that truth to us.

We have just come off a passage that in many ways reminded us of our own weakness and hypocrisy, and now Jesus shifts His focus while He continues the same thought. As we sit in the weakness that is revealed in the previous passage, we are reminded that we are needy people. And before the disciples could even voice that need, Jesus speaks into it. He knows our need, and He knows that we will have requests, so He answers that sense of need with a promise.

Ask, and it will be given. Seek, and you will surely find. Knock, and the door will be opened before you. Perhaps our first instinct is to figure out this magic formula so that we can get anything we desire, but that is not the point of the passage. On the heels of a sermon that has been reminding us of our weakness and teaching us to treasure the things of God and not the things of earth, our hearts are pointed toward what Jesus is speaking of here. When we are living with kingdom-focus and we are people that have been transformed by this message of Christ, our requests will be quite different as well. We do not ask for things that please our flesh or things of only temporal value; our requests will be gospel-focused and will be centered in the will of God. And God will answer every request that aligns with His will.

But if we are going to ask for things that align with God's will, we are going to have to know it. So how do we do that? If we want to know God's will, we must open His Word. His will is found in His Word. In this sermon alone, we have seen so much of what God's will is for His children. We are to be poor in spirit, we are to mourn for our sin, we are to be humble and meek, we are to hunger and thirst after righteousness, and the list goes on. God's will for His children is to be sanctified. We are to be more like Him. When we ask for Him to transform us into these things, He will answer.

Jesus further explains His message with a vivid illustration. He points us to a father and child, and points out that even an earthly father who is a sinful and fallen human desires to give only good things to his children. He uses this illustration to remind us that as believers, God is our Heavenly Father (John 1:12-13, Romans 8:15). If earthly fathers want to give good things to their children, how much more our perfect Heavenly Father. Our perfect Father will give us good things. He will not give us anything that is not good for us. *Let that sink into your heart.* Everything that He has given to you is good. *Everything.* Even the things that do not feel good in the moment. Even the things that you do not understand. Everything that He gives is good for us. So if we have not received it from Him—it wasn't good for us. This promise goes both ways, and it should encourage our heart from every angle. If we ask according to His will, He will give it to us (1 John 5:14-15). If we ask for something that would not be good for us, in love, He will withhold it from us. And that is just as sweet a promise for us as His children. He will give us only good things. The truth is that we don't always know what we need. He knows what we need, and He always gives it.

The golden rule follows quickly, and it is a reminder again of how Jesus calls us to live life in the upside-down kingdom. Jesus could have commanded like many other world religions the negative version of this command, for us to not do what we don't want others to do to us, but instead, Jesus calls us to a higher standard. He calls for us to do to others what we would desire for them to do to us. We extend mercy because He has extended mercy to us. We love because He has loved us.

So this Christian life is one of constantly asking, seeking, and knocking. It is one of opening His Word and learning what His will is for us. Jesus isn't just calling us to pray hurried prayers requesting what we desire, but to live a life of seeking Him.

In the original languages the words "ask," "seek," and "knock" convey continuous activity. What do you think it looks like to live a life of constantly asking, seeking, and knocking?

Based on what we have already seen Jesus teach in the Sermon on the Mount, what kind of things do you think we should be asking Him for?

When Jesus explains how a father gives good things to his children, He uses the phrase "how much more." He uses almost an identical phrase in Matthew 6:25-31. Read those verses and record what the two passages together teach us about how God relates to His children.

122

Ask, and it will be given to you. Seek, and you will find. Knock, and the door will be opened to you.

MATTHEW 7:7

WEEKLY REFLECTION

WEEK FIVE

Read Matthew 6:19-7:12

▶▶ *Paraphrase the passage from this week.*

▶▶ *What did you observe from this week's text about God and His character?*

▶▶ *What does the passage teach about the condition of mankind and about yourself?*

▶▶ *How does this passage point to the gospel?*

▶▶ *How should you respond to this passage? What is the personal application?*

▶▶ *What specific action steps can you take this week to apply the passage?*

The
NARROW WAY

WEEK SIX // DAY ONE

MATTHEW 7:13-14

We have come to the point in the sermon where the body of the sermon has finished, and Jesus moves on to the conclusion and application of the powerful words that He has just spoken. Gospel-centered preaching and Bible study must never end without a call to action. So here Jesus begins His call to action, as He calls for us to make a choice about which path we will take in this life. There are only two options presented. The wide path is the way of the world, and the narrow path is the life that Jesus has described in His sermon. Each of us has set before us the narrow way or the wide way, and we must choose which one we will enter.

Jesus is challenging His disciples to a different path. It is not the easiest path, but it is the only path that leads to flourishing. Again, we see this theme of the upside-down kingdom, because the path that Jesus commends is not the easy way out. Jesus tells us that the easy way is the way that leads to destruction, and the way that leads to life is hard. We must remember as we read these words, the words of the beatitudes that we studied before where we learned that blessed are the poor in spirit, those who mourn, the meek and humble, those who hunger and thirst after righteousness, the merciful, the pure in heart, the peacemakers, and those that are persecuted. Blessed are the ones that choose to follow the path of the upside-down kingdom. *Blessed are those that choose to live like Jesus.* Jesus is our great example, and yet His life was not a life of ease. Choosing the right thing is very rarely the easy thing. And yet Jesus tells us here that there is abundant reward in the narrow way.

The idea of two different paths is not a new concept. In fact we find references to two different ways all throughout Scripture (Proverbs 15:19, Psalm 1:1-6, Jeremiah 21:8, Deuteronomy 11:26-28, 30:19-20). There are two paths, and we are going to have to choose which one we will follow. Jesus Himself is the gate and the way to enter into this narrow way (John 10:9). And He calls for His disciples to follow Him. Our culture does not like absolutes, and this line of thinking is often not popular in a culture that promotes the belief that there are many ways that lead to God. Jesus firmly rejects this teaching while graciously calling for all to follow Him. John Stott said, "There are according to Jesus only two ways, hard and easy (there is no middle way), entered by two gates, broad and narrow (there is no other gate), trodden by two crowds, large and small (there is no neutral group), ending in two destinations, destruction and life (there is no third alternative)." Jesus calls us to make a choice that has eternal implications. He calls us to place our faith in Him alone. He asks us to call on Him for His wisdom, and leave behind the faulty wisdom of the world

(James 1:5). He calls for us to follow Him alone. He calls for us to *surrender*.

Entering into the narrow gate and following Jesus as we see here is not a guarantee of an easy life; in fact it is a guarantee that we will face hardships and difficulty as we follow Jesus. But following Jesus is always worth it because He is the prize. The goal is not an *easy* life—the goal is an *obedient* life. And even when things in our life don't make sense, and even when our path is hard, we can trust Him. Psalm 73 is a beautiful example of what it looks like to trust God even when it doesn't make sense. In this psalm, we see the psalmist state from the start the eternal truth that God is good, and yet the majority of the psalm is full of him expressing how confused and distraught he is by the world around him. Why does God allow good things to happen to bad people, and bad things to happen to God's people? In his human intellect, he does not know the answer, but when he comes to the sanctuary to worship, he is again reminded the truth of God's goodness and compelled to praise. The narrow way may not make sense to us, but we can trust in the character of our God.

So Jesus calls us to make a choice. And it is a choice that changes *everything*. Will we follow God on the narrow way, or will we run after the world's way? With the words of this beautiful sermon echoing in our minds and hearts, we can hear the tender voice of Jesus beckon us to follow Him.

Read Psalm 1:1-6 along with today's passage and contrast the two paths that are presented. In what ways can you live in the narrow path?

Read Psalm 73. How does this psalm encourage you to trust God even when life doesn't make sense? Paraphrase the psalm to be a prayer. Start with the truth of who you know God is, then write out some things that you don't understand or are struggling with, then end with a declaration of praise and trust in God.

Today's passage is the beginning of the conclusion of the sermon, and Jesus is calling for a decision. Based on today's passage and the rest of the sermon, what does God desire to change in your life, and who does He desire you to be?

BEWARE

WEEK SIX // DAY TWO

MATTHEW 7:15-20

We have just learned about the two paths, and now Jesus begins the next section with some very strong wording as He calls us to beware of false prophets. Jesus uses what is now a familiar illustration when He describes these wolves in sheep's clothing. *So who are these false prophets and why do we need to be so cautious of them?*

A false prophet is a person that distorts and changes the gospel message. The warnings against false teachers found in the New Testament are numerous. Paul described these false teachers in Acts 20:29-30 as fierce wolves that would come into the church, and that certainly borrows from this language of Jesus as He describes those that would come in to draw away believers into false doctrine. This can be done by a person teaching a doctrine that is false, or by a teacher neglecting to teach what is true. But Jesus is clear with us that these false prophets are disguised. We may not immediately know that a person is a false prophet. Their message may sound good to us. They may be popular. They may seem to have it all together. False teaching can creep in by so many ways. Teachers may teach a false gospel of Jesus plus something else. A false teacher may teach that all religions are equal and all roads lead to God. A false teacher may even distort the character of God by overemphasizing certain character traits and ignoring others. Martyn Lloyd-Jones said of false teachers, "He does not say things that are obviously wrong, but he refrains from saying things that are obviously right and true." These teachings are often subtle. They may look and sound good at first, which is why we need to be on guard. A closer look at a false teacher and the long term fruit of their ministry will show that they did not preach the whole message of Scripture. We must examine not just the appearance or popularity of a teacher, but also their teachings and their character. We must look for teachers that are not only speaking the truth, but also demonstrating the fruit of the Spirit in their lives.

Some false teachers we will be able to easily spot, but others will be far more subtle. So in order for us to be able to discern between good and bad teachers, we must know God's Word. Hebrews 5:11-14 shows us that discernment is something that is learned and that it takes root in our life when we are feeding on God's Word. The more we know God's Word, the more we will be able to discern the false teaching that is so prevalent in our culture just as it was in Jesus' day. I have often heard the illustration of the way that detectives are trained to find counterfeit money. They must study the authentic and true pieces so that they can quickly spot the counterfeits. This is true of us as believers as we study God's Word. We must know Scripture and the gospel so well that we can spot the counterfeit gospels that seek to distort our view. This will not happen instantly, but it is a process of growing in God's Word so that we can easily spot error that so subtly creeps in. The Bible is our standard of truth. There is no other measure than God's Word that we should hold our every thought and every teaching up against.

Jesus is again reminding us of one of the themes of the Sermon on the Mount, that He is more concerned about who we *are* than about what we *do*. Jesus wants transformed hearts, not just outward appearances that seem to have it all together. This warning of Jesus should compel us to know Him more through His Word so that we will be able to discern the teaching and teachers that we encounter.

*What do you think the fruit of a false teacher would be?
What about the fruit of a disciple?*

We must remember that the Christian life is a battle and stay aware of the schemes of our enemy. Read Ephesians 6:10-20 and write down our weapons against our enemy.

*Hebrews 5:11-14 describes how we can grow in discernment.
How can you practically grow in discernment?*

To
KNOW HIM

WEEK SIX // DAY THREE

MATTHEW 7:21-23

These three short verses contain some of the most sobering words in all of Scripture. In these verses, we see that some will come to the end of their life and think that they will enter the kingdom of heaven, and Jesus will say to them that He never knew them. These words of Jesus propel us back to the beginning of the sermon where we were told who would enter the kingdom. Jesus is far more concerned about who we are than what we say or do. This has been the focus of the entire sermon and it is the focus of this passage as well.

Things aren't always what they seem. There are those that do many good works, and say all the right things, but they do not know the Savior. This is what Jesus warns against in these short verses and in much of the Sermon on the Mount. Jesus had spent much time speaking of the scribes and Pharisees who did many wonderful things without knowing Him, and now He is bringing it even closer to home as He tells us that there will be those who call Him Lord, but never knew Him. We may be tempted to look at these verses and think that there are things that we must do in order to be saved, but Jesus is showing us that there is nothing we can do to earn His grace. Those that came were sure that they would enter the kingdom of heaven based on their knowledge about God and the good works they had done in His name, but Jesus again points them to the truth that those things do not determine their destiny. We must know Him, not just about Him. We must be known of Him as one of His children.

Jesus is contrasting here for us empty words and good deeds versus faith-centered, grace-driven obedience. We do not serve God to earn His favor; we serve God because we have been showered in His favor. Salvation is by grace alone, through faith alone. Saving faith is not just recognizing that Jesus is Lord. James 2:19 tells us that even the demons believe that Jesus is God. The demons believe and tremble before Him, but they are not redeemed. Salvation is not just about intellectual ascent—it is about hearts transformed by grace. Throughout the Sermon on the Mount and specifically in the Beatitudes, Jesus repeatedly pulled our attention to the truth that the heart is what matters. He is more concerned with our hearts than with the good things we do before men. *This is the upside-down kingdom.* That sinners will be made children of God, and that those that live lives full of good works done in their own strength are not God's people. It is a heavy message, but also one of great hope. It is heavy, because it causes us to examine our own hearts. But it is full of hope because God saves from every type of person those that place their faith in His saving grace. God's people are rich and poor, men and women, they come from every ethnicity and every social strata and they are united by His grace.

The heart is what matters. So we are pointed back to the Beatitudes and again prompted to examine our own hearts. These verses describe the heart of the redeemed. Do they describe us? Certainly, we will never perfectly live up to them, but for the child of God, this is what God is working and growing in us to make us more like Himself. The fate of the people Jesus speaks of had nothing to do with the good things they had done or even that they claimed to be Christians. It had to do with whether or not they had entered into a relationship with God. Jesus shifts our focus off of what we have done for Him, and puts our focus on Him. *Do we know Him?* Jesus reminds us that salvation is not about what we do, but about relationship. Are we His children saved by His marvelous grace? As His children, to know Him should be our greatest focus. In Philippians 3:8-11, Paul tells us that knowing Him should be our greatest desire. Everything else is worthless compared with knowing Jesus.

The people described in this passage seem to have it all together. They say the right things, and they do respectable things. Why does Jesus say that this isn't enough?

How does Ephesians 2:8-10 shed light on this passage? Where does salvation come from? What were we created for?

Read Philippians 3:8-11 and describe what should be most important in the life of someone that has been redeemed?

The WISE MAN and The FOOLISH MAN

WEEK SIX // DAY FOUR

MATTHEW 7:24-27

We have come to Jesus' final words of this sweeping sermon. The last words of the sermon are a warning and exhortation, and they are a call to action for every person that hears or reads these words. The conclusion of the sermon begins with a call to all who have listened, because this great sermon demands a response. We have heard the words of Jesus, and we should leave changed. In the Sermon on the Mount, Jesus has set before us the answer to the problems that lie before us, and He calls us to decision and action.

Jesus closes with one final illustration of a wise man who builds his house on the rock and when the storms come, his house is firm and secure. Jesus contrasts the wise man with a foolish man who builds his house on the sand, and it is destroyed when the storms come. Jesus is telling us to be the wise man and to forsake the way of the foolish man. The contrast of the wise man and the foolish man reminds us again of Psalm 1 speaking of the blessed man and the wicked man. Jesus is telling us that there are two paths, and we are going to have to choose which path we will take. The houses may have looked nearly identical to those that looked on, but the coming storms would reveal the truth about these two houses.

There are only two options, and every person will make a choice. Will you hear the message of the gospel and answer its call, or will you do things your own way? The path that God has called His people to is not always the easy path. Being a follower of Jesus does not mean that there will not be storms, but it means that we do not face the storms alone. He is with us every step of the way. If we are built upon Jesus who is the Solid Rock, we will be sustained through every storm, every trial, and every temptation. The storms will come, but the child of God will not be alone.

The foolish man thinks that he can handle life on his own. He thinks that he does not need God. The gospel reminds us that we cannot do it on our own. From the fall in Genesis 3, man has not been able to do it on his own. We are fallen. We are sinful. The wise man knows this truth. But the wise man is not left without hope. The wise man knows that the gospel changes everything. The message of redemption and hope that is found in Jesus gives us hope. As we fall on His love and grace, we are redeemed from our sin and ourselves. The wise man has hope in the storm, because of Jesus.

The work of sanctification is not an easy road, but it is the road that transforms us into His image (Romans 12:1-2). The storms are going to come, but even the storms are viewed through the lenses of the gospel. Though suffering will come, we have confidence that this "momentary affliction" will be overshadowed by the bright light of His radiant glory. We do not simply live for the here and now; we live for the eternal (2 Corinthians 4:7-18). The gospel gives us hope that life is bigger than today. *Victory is coming. Victory is sure.*

The gospel changes *everything*. And the Sermon on the Mount is the message of a life centered on the gospel. Jesus compels us to live for what matters. He compels us to build on solid rock so that when the storms come, we will be safe and secure in Him. May we be like the wise man that knows the message of the gospel and is changed by the gospel.

What are the differences between the wise man and the foolish man?

Both houses faced storms, and the storms revealed the hearts of the men and the stability of the houses that endured them. What are the storms that we so often face in this life?

Read 2 Corinthians 4:7-18. What do these verses tell you about how we should live and respond to the storms that come in this life?

Be Like
JESUS

WEEK SIX // DAY FIVE

MATTHEW 7:28-29

The great sermon has come to a close, and the chapter ends with Matthew telling us that the people that had gathered were astonished by the teaching of Jesus and the character of Jesus. Jesus had started the sermon speaking to His disciples, but it is clear that a great crowd had gathered to hear these famous words heralded from a mountaintop. In these short chapters, Jesus has described life in the kingdom of God. He has described what a believer should look like. *The sermon is Jesus Himself.* He is calling us as His children to be like Him. He calls us to be poor in spirit, mourners, meek, to have a hunger and thirst for righteousness, to be merciful, pure in heart, and to be persecuted for righteousness' sake. He calls us to be the light of the world and the salt of the earth. He describes how we should respond to those around us and how we should interact with our Father in heaven. This is a call to sanctification—a call for the believer to be transformed into the image of Jesus Himself.

The crowds left astonished. The Greek could even be translated as "dumbfounded." The people that left that day knew that they had seen something, and even more *someone*, that was unlike anything they had seen or heard before. They had seen Jesus. They saw a man speak with the authority of God, because He is God. They were not just astonished at His message, they were astonished by who He is. Jesus not only teaches about the law, He fulfills it. Jesus not only teaches about life, He gives it. Jesus would pour out abundant life on all who would come to Him in faith.

The sermon took place on a mountain where Jesus described the gospel-centered life to His disciples and a crowd that gathered, and it would be on another mountain that Jesus would give a great commission for His people to spread the message of the gospel and the kingdom. He has given us this same mission as well.

The message of Jesus left the crowds astonished and it should do the same for us. We should stand amazed at the man who is so much more than just a man. Jesus is the fulfillment of every promise and the hope of all the world. This glimpse of Jesus is meant to compel us to action. We are not told what the response was of the crowd that day, and perhaps this was done intentionally so that we would not so much focus on the response of the crowd that day, but on the response of our own hearts to this message. *Will we answer His call? Will we allow Him to transform us into His image? Will we become poor in spirit so that we can be lavished in the riches of His grace? Will we mourn for our sin, and be comforted by who He is? Will we be meek and humble, and trust that His plan is good for us? Will we hunger and thirst for His righteousness that satisfies every longing? Will we extend mercy because of the mercy that has been extended to us? Will we be pure in heart and follow God with a single-minded focus on His glory? Will we endure rejection for His name? Will we live our life in this upside-down kingdom where the last are first and joy comes from laying your life down? Will we be like Jesus?*

Read the entire Sermon on the Mount again. What stands out to you most from your study of this teaching of Jesus?

What does the Sermon on the Mount tell us about who Jesus is?

What does the Sermon on the Mount tell us about who we should be?

When Jesus had finished saying these things, the crowds were astonished at his teaching, because he was teaching them like one who had authority, and not like their scribes.

MATTHEW 7:28–29

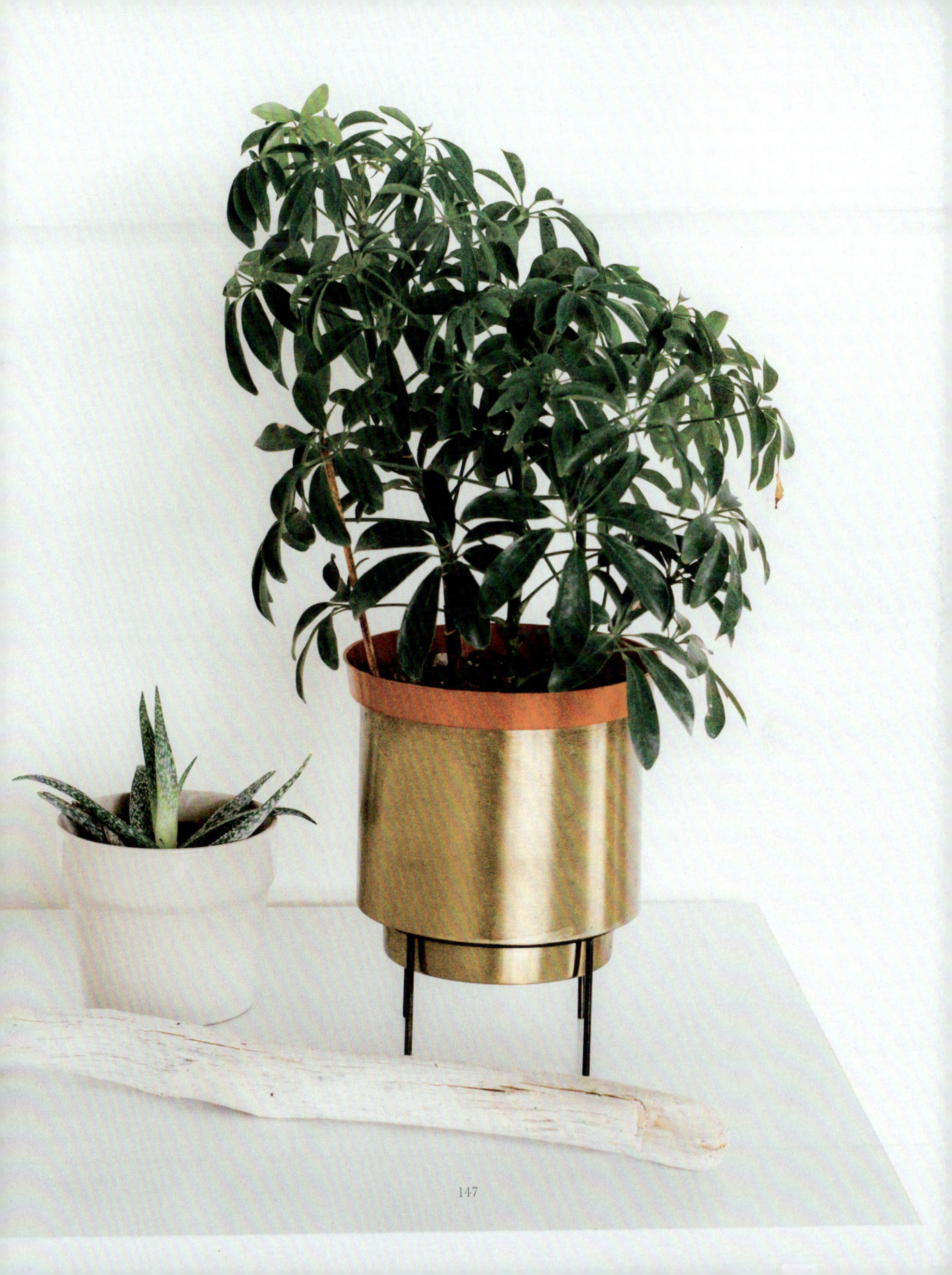

WEEKLY REFLECTION

WEEK SIX

Read Matthew 7:13-7:29

▶▶ *Paraphrase the passage from this week.*

▶▶ *What did you observe from this week's text about God and His character?*

▶▶ *What does the passage teach about the condition of mankind and about yourself?*

▶▶ *How does this passage point to the gospel?*

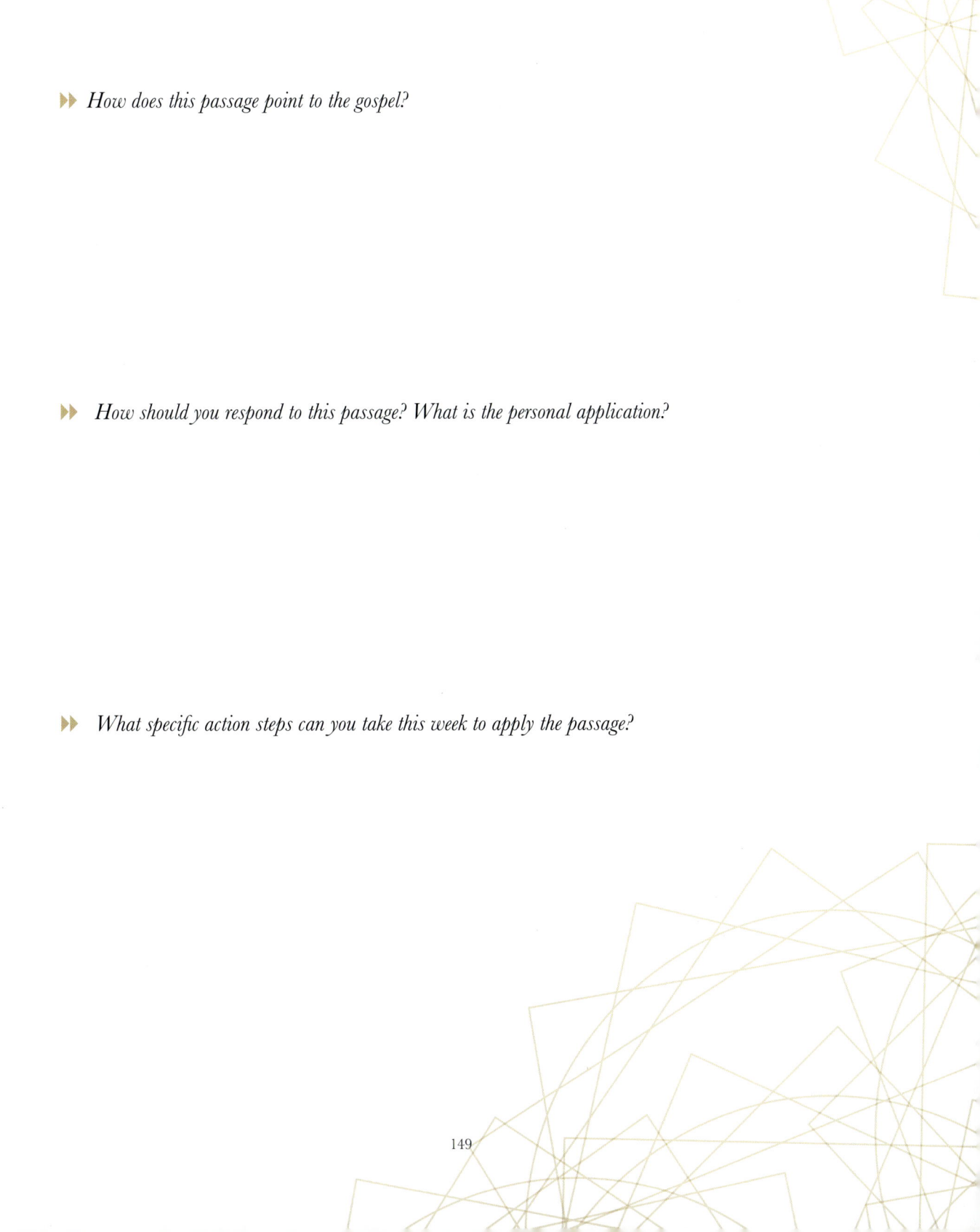

▶▶ *How should you respond to this passage? What is the personal application?*

▶▶ *What specific action steps can you take this week to apply the passage?*

WHAT IS THE GOSPEL?

Thank you for reading and enjoying this study with us! We are abundantly grateful for the Word of God, the instruction we glean from it, and the ever-growing understanding about God's character from it. We're also thankful that Scripture continually points to one thing in innumerable ways: the gospel.

We remember our brokenness when we read about the fall of Adam and Eve in the garden of Eden (Genesis 3), when sin entered into a perfect world and maimed it. We remember the necessity that something innocent must die to pay for our sin when we read about the atoning sacrifices in the Old Testament. We read that we have all sinned and fallen short of the glory of God (Romans 3:23), and that the penalty for our brokenness, the wages of our sin, is death (Romans 6:23). We all are in need of grace, mercy, and most importantly—we all need a Savior.

We consider the goodness of God when we realize that He did not plan to leave us in this dire state. We see His promise to buy us back from the clutches of sin and death in Genesis 3:15. And we see that promise accomplished with Jesus Christ on the cross. Jesus Christ knew no sin yet became sin so that we might become righteous through His sacrifice (2 Corinthians 5:21.) Jesus was tempted in every way that we are and lived sinlessly. He was reviled, yet still yielded Himself for our sake, that we may have life abundant in Him. Jesus lived the perfect life that we could not live, and died the death that we deserved.

The gospel is profound yet simple. There are many mysteries in it that we can never exhaust this side of heaven, but there is still overwhelming weight to its implications in this life. The gospel is the telling of our sinfulness and God's goodness, and this gracious gift compels a response. We are saved by grace through faith, (Ephesians 2:9) which means that we rest with faith in the grace that Jesus Christ displayed on the cross. We cannot save ourselves from our brokenness or do any amount of good works to merit God's favor, but we can have faith that what Jesus accomplished in His death, burial, and resurrection was more than enough for our salvation and our eternal delight. When we accept God, we are commanded to die to our self and our sinful desires and live a life worthy of the calling we have received (Ephesians 4:1). The gospel compels us to be sanctified, and in so doing, we are conformed to the likeness of Christ Himself.

This is hope. This is redemption. This is the gospel.

*He made the one who did
not know sin to be sin for us,
so that in him we might become
the righteousness of God.*

2 CORINTHIANS 5:21

Thank you

FOR STUDYING GOD'S
WORD WITH US!

CONNECT WITH US:

@THEDAILYGRACECO

@KRISTINSCHMUCKER

CONTACT US:

INFO@THEDAILYGRACECO.COM

SHARE:

#THEDAILYGRACECO

#LAMPANDLIGHT

WEBSITE:

WWW.THEDAILYGRACECO.COM